SURVIVAL
HACKS

SURVIVAL HACKS

OVER 200 WAYS TO USE EVERYDAY ITEMS
FOR WILDERNESS SURVIVAL

CREEK STEWART, author of *Build the Perfect Bug Out Bag*

Adams Media

New York   London   Toronto   Sydney   New Delhi

Adams Media
An Imprint of Simon & Schuster, Inc.
100 Technology Center Drive
Stoughton, MA 02072

For information about special discounts for bulk purchases, please contact Simon & Schuster Special Sales at 1-866-506-1949 or business@simonandschuster.com.

The Simon & Schuster Speakers Bureau can bring authors to your live event. For more information or to book an event contact the Simon & Schuster Speakers Bureau at 1-866-248-3049 or visit our website at www.simonspeakers.com.

Interior art by Eric Andrews.

Manufactured in the United States of America

20 2024

Library of Congress Cataloging-in-Publication Data has been applied for.

ISBN 978-1-4405-9334-5
ISBN 978-1-4405-9334-2 (ebook)

Contents

Introduction

sur-VIV-al HACK-ing
verb
The act of using what you have to get what you need to stay alive in any situation.

"Hacking" is making do with what you've got. It has three aspects:

1. Using knowledge of basic survival principles
2. Innovative thinking
3. Exploiting available resources

KNOWLEDGE OF BASIC SURVIVAL PRINCIPLES

Knowledge is the basis for almost every successful survival skill. You can get it from reading books, listening to the advice and stories of others, and watching the actions of others. However, the most important way to gain true knowledge of survival principles is trial and error with your own two hands. No method of learning takes the place of hands-on, personal experience. Your options in a survival scenario will ultimately depend on your understanding of basic survival principles that surround shelter, water, fire, and food.

INNOVATIVE THINKING

I've often said that *innovation* is the most important survival skill. Innovation can be defined in survival as *creatively using available resources to execute a plan formulated using pre-existing survival knowledge*. At the end of the day, the application of survival principles is only limited by your ability to creatively use them.

EXPLOITING AVAILABLE RESOURCES

Available resources are anything natural or manmade, from leaves and sticks to trash bottles and windshield wipers. Everything is potentially a survival resource that you can exploit, with knowledge and creativity, to get what you need. In this book, we explore hundreds of everyday items that can be modified, repurposed, reused, reshaped, rebuilt, or recycled to meet some kind of basic human survival need.

THREE THOUSAND FAILURES

Some of the hacks featured in this book are tips and tricks I've absorbed throughout my lifelong study of survival; I learned them from other people and from watching others in the field. I've picked up all sorts of hacks from friends, family, students, and other survival enthusiasts. I'm always on the lookout for a fun, new, and creative survival hack.

However, many of the following 200-plus survival hacks are also the result of more than 3,000 failed attempts. Some, such as the Make a Fire Pipe hack in Chapter 3, took more than 20 tries to get right. If I had quit working on a hack idea at the first failed attempt, this book would be about five pages long.

The 200-plus hacks listed in the following pages are proven to work. I've successfully practiced them all. Each of them is an actionable lesson in survival; you can go into your backyard and practice them right now. Many can be executed in the comfort of your home or garage, and certainly you can use them on your next camping trip.

THE MORE YOU HACK

As you study, practice, and use these 200-plus hacks from everyday objects, you're bound to learn more about survival principles and how to creatively meet basic survival needs. This knowledge will lead to new "hack" ideas that I want to hear about! E-mail your hack ideas to *creek@creekstewart.com*. Who knows, your hack could make it into the next volume of *Survival Hacks*.

Chapter 1

Shelter Hacks

In extreme conditions, you can survive as few as 3 hours without shelter. Exposure to the elements is almost always your number one survival priority. Keeping warm, cool, dry, or protected from the rain, snow, and wind is easier said than done when you're working with limited resources. You may need some creative hacking in order to be effective.

I'll never forget the words of a wise Scoutmaster when I was a kid: "Boys, the ability to dress yourselves is the first of all great survival lessons." He was right. Shelter starts with clothing and footwear. It ends with more complicated principles such as windbreaks, insulation, bedding, roofing materials, fire reflection, and waterproofing.

This chapter's hacks are all designed to help offer protection for you and your gear from your biggest survival adversary—the weather. Without protection from the elements, few other survival priorities matter. The ability to cope with what the weather throws at you is what keeps you alive long enough in order to even execute other survival skills directed toward water, fire, or food. We'll start this chapter of shelter hacks in the spirit of my old Scoutmaster—with clothing.

A BELT WITH TRACTION

A broken belt in the field can be a devastating setback, especially if you're using your belt to carry gear such as a knife, your everyday carry (EDC) kit, and saw. A surprisingly simple and very durable hack belt can be made from the tread of an old bicycle tire. When the walls are trimmed away until just the face tread remains, it becomes the perfect belt width. Staple, rivet, or lash one end to your buckle, punch holes in the other end for adjusting, and you've got a belt that will last a lifetime. You can also use bicycle tire treads as suspenders, pack straps, replacement handles, and rifle slings. Slivers from the rubber tread can even be used as harsh-weather fire starters.

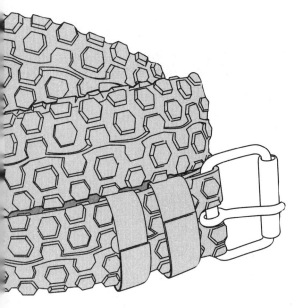

PANTYHOSE PREVENTION

An old hunting buddy introduced me to this unique hack, and I've never forgotten it. As manly as he was, he wore pantyhose every time he hunted—both in summer and winter. During hot summer months, he swore that the pantyhose barrier made it impossible for ticks to latch onto the skin. In cold temps, pantyhose make a very effective base layer. It's all about layering in cold weather, and the addition of a few pairs of pantyhose to your cold-weather car kit is a great idea that's easy on the wallet. If you're using a new pair of boots, pantyhose can also help prevent blisters by reducing the friction from your shoe. Simply trim off the feet and wear them as a sock liner.

LIP BALM ZIPPER WATERPROOFER

In extreme weather, even the slightest nonwaterproofed area or seam can become a huge setback and source of frustration. Many zippers are water repellent because of their construction, but they are not waterproof. One way to help waterproof jacket and backpack zippers is to run lip balm with firm pressure along the length of the zipper. Wax from the lip balm will press into the cracks and prevent water from seeping in. This will also help to lubricate the zippers (especially metal ones) and make them easier to use. Other products that can work for this in a pinch are crayons, candles, some hair pomades, and beeswax. The wax will wear off with use, but is a great temporary fix when Mother Nature proves to be unmerciful.

HANDY TOOL/GEAR GRIPS

Places and ways to secure gear and tools should be a part of every survival wardrobe. Here is a quick hack using bicycle inner tubes to secure a variety of tools and gear to belts, backpack straps, knife sheaths, and even walking sticks. Crosscut sections of bicycle inner tubes are widely known within the survival community as Ranger bands. When these sections of inner tubes are threaded onto belts or backpack shoulder straps, they make secure grips for a variety of small gear that you wish to quickly access. I keep a multitool right on my backpack strap, using Ranger band gear grips to hold it securely in place. These grips are weatherproof, inexpensive, and very strong. They can also be used as an effective fire tinder in bad weather.

ROYCROFT PACK

Canadian survival instructor Tom Roycroft was tasked by the Canadian Department of National Defence to come up with improvised backpack ideas that soldiers could construct with limited resources in the field. He ultimately invented what is known as the Roycroft pack. Lash a simple triangle of limbs together as shown. The left and right sides are the length of your armpit to your fingertip. The bottom is the length of your elbow to fingertip. Lay any kind of fabric, sheeting, or jacket on top of the frame and place your supplies in the middle. Fold the remaining fabric inward; a crisscross lashing holds everything in place. Finally, tie a lark's head knot on top and run the 2 rope ends around the bottom corners and tie them at your waist. You can make this pack in just a few minutes with hardly any resources.

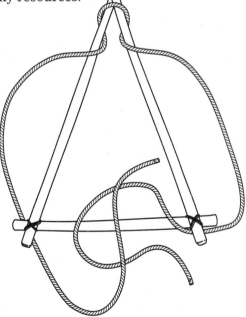

TUMPLINE FOR HEAVY LOADS

Here is an old hack for carrying heavy loads that you may
not have seen before. I first learned of this trick when
studying the mountain men fur traders of the 1800s.
Mountain men would have to carry heavy loads of fur pelts
along hiking paths and canoe portages. They did this
almost exclusively using a tumpline, a strap that runs over
the shoulders and around the top of the head. The ends of
the tumpline are attached to the sides of the basket or pack
you're carrying. It sounds very awkward, but in fact it
allows you to carry a lot of cargo with less effort.
The tumpline aligns the weight along your spine rather
than weighing down your shoulders like a traditional
backpack. It is important to note that the tumpline should
wrap across the top of
your head with you
leaning forward
rather than across
the forehead.

SOCK HALF GLOVES

A wise woodsman wears a scarf around his neck in cold weather. Much of your heat is lost through the thinly insulated veins and arteries that run through the neck. The same is true for the wrist. Heat is lost through the blood being close to the skin as it works its way to and from the fingers. For this reason, half gloves (also called wrist gloves) that insulate the wrist can make a huge difference in keeping your fingers warm in cold weather. You can make a very effective pair of half gloves from the leg and cuff portion of a pair of old wool hiking socks. Cut the sock off above the ankle, trim a hole for your thumb, and pull it on. This half glove will insulate much of the palm, the exposed veins on the back of the hand, and your wrist.

SEAL YOUR SEAMS WITH TOILET RINGS

I'm a huge fan of leather boots. However, they require a lot of maintenance. During extended periods in wet environments, many leather boots will leak at the seams. I have a quick and easy hack for that, and it uses an inexpensive wax toilet bowl seal ring. Before heading outside, heat the seams of your boots with a candle. Don't burn them or catch them on fire, just heat them up. While the seams are still hot, use a cloth to rub some wax from the toilet ring along them. The wax will melt and draw into the seam, making it nearly impermeable to water. Even in a bug out or survival scenario, wax toilet rings are always available. You can also use this method to waterproof the entire boot. Just warm the boots first by letting them sit in the sun or near a fire.

NEWSPAPER MUKLUKS

Mukluks are traditional soft-soled boots originating in the Arctic. The design is most functional in extreme cold conditions when the snow is soft and powdery as opposed to wet and slushy. Mukluks allow the feet to breathe through thick layers of insulation and, like their moccasin cousins, offer very quiet travel. You can make a hack pair of mukluks by laying out 20–30 sheets of newspaper flat on the floor with a corner facing forward. Place your foot in the middle with your toes pointing toward the outside corner and then fold each of the 4 corners in on top and across your foot. Tape or lash this layer into place. Next, fold a towel in half, place it on the floor, and wrap it around the foot in the exact same fashion using rope or tape. A final layer of tarp, scrap jacket material, or canvas can be layered on the outside for added weather protection. Add more layers of newspaper for more insulation.

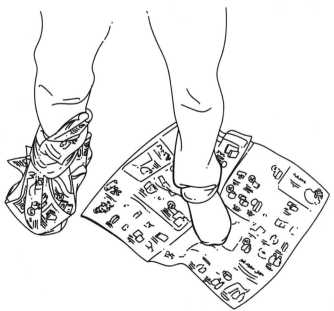

RACKET SNOWSHOES

Deep snow can be a devastating setback to a traveling survivor. Luckily, necessity is the mother of invention, and you can make snowshoes from many different items. One of the quickest snowshoe hacks that I've used is a pair of tennis rackets. Loop leather or rope foot straps around the strings of a tennis racket and lash them around your boot for a very comfortable fit. The heel of the boot should be left to move freely for ease of walking. The lashings should form an X pattern across the top of the boot with at least 1 line wrapping around the back of your boot to hold the foot firmly in place.

SCRAP RUBBER HUARACHES

The Tarahumara people of Mexico are world renowned for their ability to run long distances. What's even more interesting is that they often run these distances in improvised minimalist sandals called huaraches. You can make huaraches from a piece of cord and scrap rubber taken from a car mat or even a tire.

First, trace your foot on the rubber and make a mark between your big toe and second toe where the toe thong will go. Next, cut the traced soles from the rubber and punch a hole on each side just near the back of the arch of your foot. Then punch another one on your mark for the toe thong. Cut a 6' length of cord and feed it through the toe thong hole with a knot on the other end to hold it in place. Feed the working end through the outside hole, around your heel, through the other hole, around the string on the top of your foot, and then retrace the lashing to lace the sandal in place.

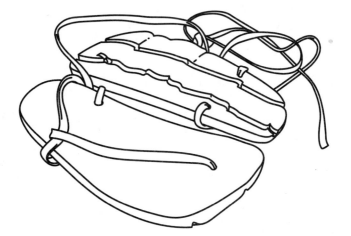

THIS INSOLE NEVER *FELT* SO GOOD

If you follow my work at all, then you already know that I love wool. It's amazing in cold weather, and there's nothing like a good pair of wool socks to keep your feet warm and toasty when the temperature plummets. One quick and easy footwear hack that I've used over the years to give me that extra edge of warmth and comfort is to custom cut my own boot insoles from wool felt. Felt is a fabric made by matting and compressing wool fibers until they become a solid piece of material. You can buy wool felt at almost any fabric store. Trace your existing shoe insoles on the felt to get the right size, cut the felt out with scissors, and insert them into your hiking boots. Not only will they add an extra layer of comfort, but the wool will also provide much-needed insulation for the bottom of your feet against the cold ground.

USE ICE TO MAKE YOUR SHOES MORE COMFORTABLE

There are many reasons why your boots can feel smaller than usual. Maybe you've put on weight. Maybe you've decided to wear thicker socks. Maybe your boots got soaked and shrank when they dried. For whatever reason, there is a quick and easy way to stretch them out a little bit. Fill resealable freezer bags about three-quarters full with water. Stuff those water bags into your boots and put them in the freezer. As the bags of water freeze they will expand and force your boot to stretch. Freezing water has the power to burst concrete; this hack is a great way to use that power to do something that is very difficult to do—stretch your boots!

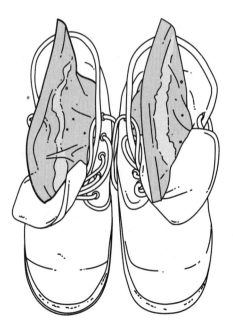

DUCT TAPE SNOWSHOES

If a pair of tennis rackets aren't handy, here is another great snowshoe hack that only takes a few minutes longer to hack into existence. Cut and bend a ½" diameter flexible green sapling into a teardrop shape, approximately 2' × 1'. Use duct tape at the intersection to hold it together. Use more of the tape to create a web-like netting that spans the width and length of the wooden frame's interior space. This will resemble a crude wood and duct tape version of a tennis racket head. Next, duct-tape 2 braces across the top that span the distance from the ball of your foot to your heel. These should be 1" in diameter and cut from green wood. Finally, use duct tape to secure the front of your boot to the front wooden cross brace. Your heel should lift freely upward but rest securely on the rear brace when stepping down.

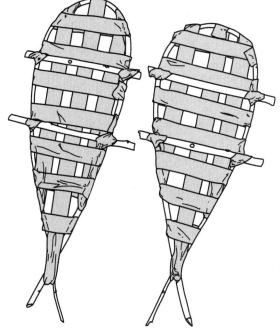

SOCK GAITERS

This hack isn't as much about shoes as it is stopping things from getting inside them while you're on the move. I rarely spend time in the woods (especially the desert) without a pair of gaiters lashed around my shins. Gaiters are a protective garment designed to keep mud, snow, thorns, sand, forest debris, and insects from getting into your boots while hiking. They also protect your shins against thorns, some kinds of snakebites, branch slaps, and moisture. Some good friends of mine went on a mission trip to Belize. While watching a video of their experience I noticed that their guides were wearing makeshift sock gaiters. They'd tucked their pant legs in their boots. Then they took the cut-off portions of the legs from thick hunting socks and pulled that up and around the ankle of their boot. Several of them even had a front section of a 2-liter bottle cut and tucked inside the gaiter for added protection.

TRASH BAG SHELTER

You've probably heard of using a trash bag as a poncho. However, not only can a trash bag be an incredible poncho, but it can serve as a surprisingly effective one-person shelter as well. As a kid I was taught to cut a head hole in the middle of the bottom of the bag and poke my arms out of 2 more holes cut at the corners. Wow, was this wrong! You only want to make a 2" cut about 1' down the fold from one of the bottom corners. When you make this cut across the fold it ends up being double that length when you open it up. This is your face hole. Pull the bag over your head and stretch the hole over your face and under your chin. Tuck your legs inside and sit against a downwind side of a big tree to get some rest.

HACK TARP BOAT

This hack isn't about making shelter but rather using a shelter tarp to make an improvised boat.

1. Lay your tarp flat on the ground. I used a 9' × 12' tarp.
2. Pile pine boughs or leafy branches in a circle about 12" high. This will be the diameter of your boat. Leave at least 1'–2' of tarp around the perimeter.
3. Lay a grid of sturdy sticks, 1"–2" in diameter, on top of the circle.
4. Pile another 12" of green boughs on top, again in a circular pattern.
5. Wrap the tarp around the circle and tie it to the grid of sticks.
6. Cross your fingers.

   See the complete photo series of steps at *http://willow havenoutdoor.com/hack-tarp-boat/.*

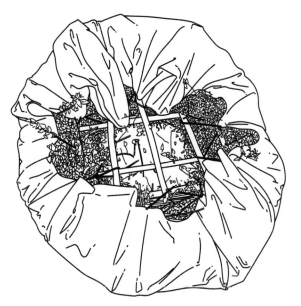

POP CAN SNOW/SAND ANCHOR

Securing tent or canopy stakes in snow or sand can be very difficult, if not impossible. You can make a very simple and easy snow/sand anchor from a flattened soda can. Start by flattening the can sideways, not from top to bottom. Next, punch a hole in the middle of the flattened can. Feed your tent guyline through the hole and place a knot on the other side to hold it secure. Finally, bury the flattened can in the sand or snow. The flat face of the buried can will act as an anchor to hold your line secure. Almost anything flat and sturdy will work, but a flattened pop can is an easy hack.

POP TAB TENSIONER

One of the first skills I teach in all of my survival courses is how to tie up an effective canopy shelter. Not only does this portion of the course involve canopy configurations, but I also teach tensioning knots such as the taut-line hitch. If the wrong tensioning knots are used, a canopy shelter can come crashing down when you least expect it. One great hack for tightening guylines is to use a plain old aluminum pop can tab. Once you remove it from the can, break off the tiny little metal ring that holds it to the can. This will expose a jagged edge that's critical for this hack to work. Now feed your line through the tab as shown, and it can be used to tighten or loosen guylines as needed without having to fuss with knots.

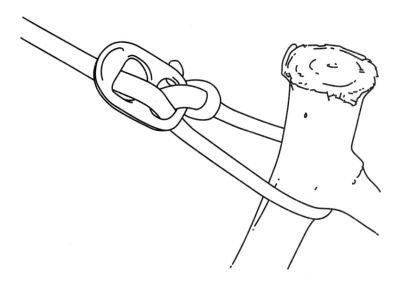

TWO SIMPLE GROMMET SAVERS

Grommets on the corners of tarps are notorious for tearing out in high winds and storms. A simple hack to help prevent this from happening is to thread your guyline through the grommet and then around a small, stout stick. Tying around this stick distributes the stress on the grommet to a larger surface area and applies downward pressure on the grommet rather than a direct pull against it. A metal bottle cap also works very well as reinforcement. Punch a hole through the middle and tie a knot on the other side to hold it. This acts as a button stopper against the grommet and relieves stress on the grommet and tarp. *Note*: The grommets of a *tightly* stretched tarp are less likely to fail due to reduced wind flap.

DIY CANOPY ON A BUDGET

If you're a do-it-yourself type of survivalist (most of us are), you may be interested in hacking your own light-weight canopy shelter. One of the best makeshift canopy materials I've ever worked with is Tyvek house wrap. This is a waterproof and tear-resistant fabric used as a moisture barrier beneath the brick and/or siding on homes. Often, contractors will happily give scrap pieces of Tyvek material to those who ask. It is also available by the roll from home improvement hardware stores. The edges do not fray, and it is incredibly lightweight. The addition of strategically placed grommets (also available at hardware stores) will create a survival tarp canopy as good as any store-bought variety. *Note*: A dye solution made from water and black walnut husks will color Tyvek to a very proper woodsman tannish brown color.

SHOCK BAND HACK

High winds can be devastating to even the best of canopy shelters. Such shelters are like sails in high winds, and if you don't use really strong guylines (such as paracord), the lines can easily snap in surging wind gusts. When using less-than-preferred-strength guylines for canopy shelters, consider implementing a shock band along the guyline. This is a piece of rubber or bungee cord strategically placed along your guyline. In high winds, the shock band will take the brunt of the stress and keep your shelter safely in place. Overhand loops can be tied along the guyline to allow a modern bungee cord with hooks on each end to be quickly and easily installed. Strips of tire inner tube, slingshot bands, surgical tubing, and even exercise bands can be used as well.

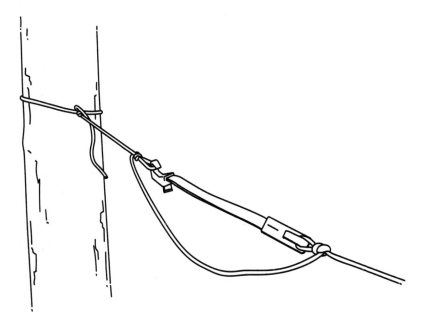

BUG OUT BICYCLE SHELTER

Bugging out on a bicycle has certain advantages. It can weave in and out of congested traffic jams, and it can't run out of gas. It can also act as an independent canopy shelter frame in the absence of trees or anchor points. While many different configurations are possible, this illustration shows a classic arrangement, using the tires as front pillars with guylines stretching to the front. A smaller canopy strung from the handlebars makes a convenient gear storage vestibule or a dry spot for firewood. See the Bicycle-Powered Slingshot hack in Chapter 4 to find out how to convert the front fork of a bicycle into a powerful small-game slingshot.

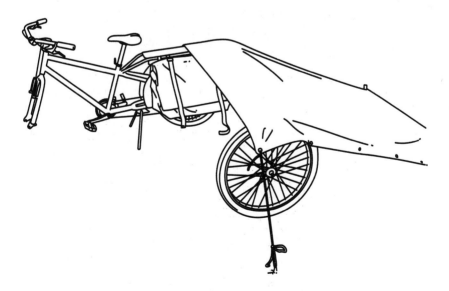

GLOW-IN-THE-DARK GUYLINES

I've seen even the most experienced woodsman trip over his canopy guylines during a late-night trip to the latrine. A careless fall over guylines can have devastating consequences in a survival scenario, including eye gouges, broken bones, sprained wrists or ankles, and pulled muscles. A very simple gear exchange can help prevent such an event: Replace dark or earth-toned guylines with glow-in-the-dark paracord. Dark guylines can be difficult to see at night even with the use of a headlamp or flashlight, but glow-in-the-dark lines are not only much more visible, but they glow even brighter when struck by a beam of light.

Bonus hack: Replace backpack zipper pulls and gear lanyards with glow-in-the-dark paracord as well to eliminate unnecessary guesswork in low-light conditions.

6" TENSIONING STICK

This is a cool trick that replaces a tensioning knot when stretching a ridgeline for a canopy shelter, rain fly, dining fly, or clothesline. It allows for quick and easy tightening (or loosening) of a rope stretched between 2 trees or anchor points.

Start by cutting a 6" stick about 1" in diameter. A wooden dowel or old broomstick works perfectly for this. Next, drill a hole through each end about the same diameter as your rope. Thread the working end of your rope through the right-hand hole and then circle the rope around the tree or anchor point. Finally, thread the rope through the other hole on the opposite end of the stick and tie a simple over-hand knot on the other side to act as a stopper. This configuration allows you to slide the stick up and down the ridgeline to tension.

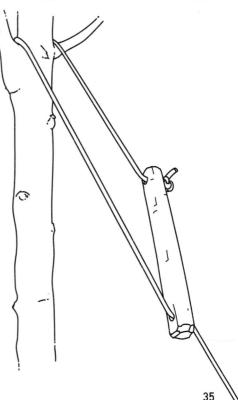

PALLET SHELTER

You can find discarded wooden pallets around almost every industrial park, dumpster area, dockyard, or retail establishment. Their durability, size, and shape make them perfect for an infinite number of shelter configurations. The quickest to erect is a simple A-frame shelter. Place a layer (or two) of pallets on the ground as a bed frame. This not only gets you off the ground and away from moisture, but it also creates dead air space that can be stuffed with insulation materials such as leaves, hay, or newspapers. Once the bed frame is finished, lean pallets on each side to meet in the middle above the bed in an A-frame shape. You can cover this structure in debris or a tarp, or even stuff the hollow interior spaces of the pallets with insulation to form semi-solid walls. Because of their panel-based construction, pallet shelters can be completed in a fraction of the time it would take to construct normal primitive shelters.

See the Pallet Bow hack in Chapter 4 for how to make a hunting bow using a pallet.

FRAMEWORK COLLAR CONNECTOR

If you need a long pole, you'll have to lash together 2 limbs or saplings for the right length. This is the case when making a dome framework for wigwam-style shelters. If cordage is in short supply, a hack using an energy bottle from your trash may be the solution.

After slicing off the top and bottom of the bottle, a very strong cylindrical tube remains. You can use this tube as a collar for connecting the ends of 2 limbs. Taper the ends so they slide into the tube opposite each other and form a snug fit when wedged together. This collar will hold them together surprisingly well and will not stretch with moisture as many lashings will. If the collar's a bit loose, heat it over coals or a flame and it will shrink and tighten the fit.

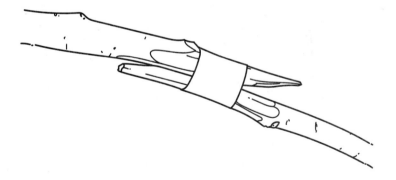

A $1 SLEEPING PAD OR FIRE REFLECTOR

Available at most dollar stores, a reflective vehicle dash-board protector can be easily repurposed into a sleeping mat with the addition of a few inches of leaves or grass underneath. It isn't thick enough to be an insulator, so the additional natural or manmade insulating materials underneath are necessary. Its construction makes it much more durable than an average emergency survival blanket, so it is also reusable and repackable. The shiny silver Mylar (designed to reflect sun rays away from a car dash) is equally effective in reflecting and recycling body heat. It can also be used as a wind block and to reflect heat from a fire when hung from the back of a shelter. When folded and rolled, this product is about the size of a pop can.

A QUICK AND DIRTY CAMP TABLE

This isn't as much a shelter hack as it is a camp furniture hack. Survival camps can be crude, and the need for furniture often arises. One of the easiest table hacks I've ever used starts with erecting a quad pod framework. Lash 4 sticks together at the top, using a tripod-style lashing. This creates a quad pod with 4 legs. Now lash 2 horizontal sticks to each side to create a very nice tabletop frame. Then lay either individual sticks, found boards, or flat plastic or metal scraps across the horizontal frame to form a table-top. This table is quick to erect, requires few materials (only rope and sticks), and can be broken down to transport if necessary. It can serve as a kitchen prep area or as a table to get gear and tools off the ground.

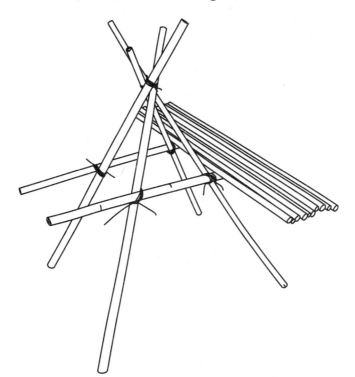

HOBO CANDLE HEATER

Even the heat from a small candle can raise the inside
temperature of a small space several degrees. You can
make a very simple hobo heater to capture and radiate that
heat even further. Place 2 terra cotta flower pots upside
down on top of each other. Make sure the bottom pot is a
bit smaller so that there is an inch or so of space between it
and the other pot. These should then be elevated slightly
above a candle. Straddling them across 2 bricks is a perfect
way to support them. The candle heats the first terra cotta
pot as well as the air space between the pots. The warm air
rises through the hole in the top
of the second pot. The terra cotta
captures, holds, and radiates
the heat longer than if the
candle was just burning in
open air.

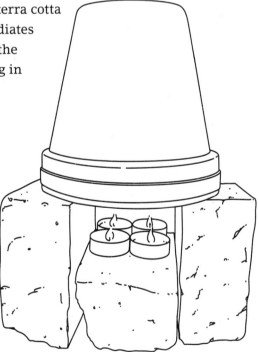

METAL BUCKET STORAGE HEATER

A storage heater is a heating system that uses electrical current to heat up ceramic bricks; these can hold and radiate the heat into a room for hours. You can make a hack storage heater from a metal bucket, sand, and some rocks or bricks. Before bedding down at night, heat some softball-sized rocks or bricks in the fire. Once piping hot, place them into a metal bucket and surround them with sand. Put the lid on the metal bucket and place it inside your shelter on a fire-resistant surface and away from the walls and bedding material. This storage heater will put off heat all night long. A heater like this is more than sufficient to cut the cold in a small shelter, and you'll be surprised at its effectiveness.

A SIMPLE BLACKOUT AIR CONDITIONER

A power outage during sweltering hot summer months can be downright deadly, especially to infants and the elderly. In a disaster scenario, travel isn't always an option, so sometimes you have to hunker down and wait things out until utilities come back online. Here is a quick and easy hack using an old Styrofoam cooler and some frozen food from the freezer to make a great little temporary blackout air conditioner. This is a hack best taught by video, so I've filmed a tutorial showing exactly how to build it. Watch the video at *www.willowhavenoutdoor.com/makeshift-emergency-air-conditioner.*

BLANKET CHAIR

Finding a good place to sit in an improvised survival camp can be very frustrating—especially when the ground is wet or snow covered. Here is a hack to improvise a very comfortable seat in just a few minutes. The only parts you need are 4 sturdy poles and a blanket or scrap piece of durable fabric. Cut 2 poles that are 6'–8' long by 1½"–2" thick and then cut a third that is the same thickness and 4' long. Lash the 2 long poles together at one end using a bipod lashing. Fold the blanket or fabric in half, bunch the end together, and suspend this end with rope from the cross at the bipod lashing. Insert the 4' pole at the unsecured fold of the blanket so that it sticks out at both ends, and rest it against the longer poles. Finally, kick back the center long pole as a chair support and lean back to relax.

BED SHEET HAMMOCK

You can construct an incredibly lightweight, packable, and durable survival hammock from a bed sheet and rope. The trick is in how to tie the ends so they don't rip out in the middle of the night. Start by accordion-folding the ends of the bed sheet on each side to meet in the middle. At this point the sheet should be in a shape resembling a banana. Now, tie a main line to the end using 2 half hitches and leave at least 8" of sheet sticking out. Fold this remaining 8" down and lash to the main sheet body using a whip knot. This creates a very strong "loop" of bed sheet material that can bear a very heavy load without tearing or ripping. See a photo series of this hack at *www.practical primitive.com/skillofthemonth/hammock.html.*

FEED SACK COT

Feed sacks and burlap bags are very strong and durable. Their tubular shape also makes them very useful when configuring a survival cot. Start by erecting 2 large tripods from 5' saplings. Next, unravel the hem along the bottom of the feed sacks (you'll need at least 2 sacks). This will create a tubular piece of fabric about 24" wide, the perfect width for a fine woodsman sleeping cot. Slide the tubular sacks over 2 7'-long sturdy saplings that have been cleared of all limbs and branches. This will create a hammock-style cot that can be stretched between the legs of the large tripods erected earlier. The front 2 legs of the tripods will support the cot on each side while pulling the feed sacks taut in the middle for comfortable "off-the-ground" sleeping.

TIRE STOOL

A stack of 3 tires makes an excellent camp stool with one very simple modification. Punch holes with your knife every 3" around the inside rim of the top tire. Weave paracord (or any strong cordage) from a hole on one side to a hole on the opposite side and create a star-shaped pattern, hopping from side to side. By the time each hole is threaded, this woven rope chair seat will be strong enough to hold an average adult man and is a much more comfortable place to sit than any log or stump dragged from the forest. If rope is unavailable, place pine boughs in a crisscross pattern atop the tire until 3" thick. These will provide enough strength to make a seat that will last many days.

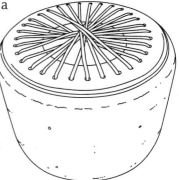

THE 3-OUNCE CAMP CHAIR

You can make a fantastic hammock-style camp chair from just a 3' × 1' piece of ripstop nylon fabric (available at any fabric store) and some 550 paracord. If you're lucky enough to camp near a tree with a stout horizontal branch, this chair style could be the perfect piece of camp furniture for you, and it all fits easily in just a jacket pocket.

Throw 2 strands of paracord over the horizontal branch and tie them to each side of the ripstop nylon. The fabric opens up and makes a perfect hammock-style seat. A similar arrangement can be made by placing a strong crossbeam across the top of 2 large tripods and hanging the chair from this beam.

Chapter 2

Water Hacks

In extreme conditions, humans can survive approximately 3 days without water. In a survival scenario the need for water is second only to regulating core body temperature. Nothing else matters if you can't supply your brain, organs, and muscles with the hydration necessary to make decisions and keep pressing forward. The human body is 50–65 percent water and is highly dependent on regular replenishments.

There is more to water in survival conditions than many people realize. First, you must find water. In some environments, like the desert, this can be an incredible challenge. Second, you must gather and contain available water. This can be difficult with limited resources. Third, you must purify and filter water so that it is safe to drink. Shortcomings in any of these categories can leave you staggering and stumbling with the effects of dehydration. Let's explore several survival water hacks using everyday items that could mean the difference between life or death.

CONDOM CANTEEN

Many survivalists, including myself, suggest packing non-lubricated condoms in survival kits. They are small, compact, and inexpensive and have a plethora of survival uses. One noteworthy function is as a compact emergency water container. However, few people have ever actually tried carrying water in one. Here are a couple tips I've learned from experience. Fill the condom in a sock to protect it during travel. Use any rigid hollow tube such as an ink pen, elderberry branch, or bamboo section as a spout and secure the base of the condom around it using duct tape or paracord. Carve a spout stopper from any dry branch and add a sling and you're ready to make tracks with more than 1 liter of drinking water.

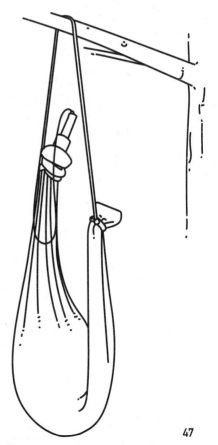

COAL-BURNED CONTAINER

Containers are a luxury in the wild. Without one, it can be very difficult to gather, contain, or boil water. The lack of metal arts didn't prevent primitive cultures from making containers. In fact, some of the first containers were "hacked" by using red-hot coals from the fire to burn depressions into chunks of wood. You can do this as well. Carefully place a coal in a small carved groove and then blow on it, using a hollow reed. The intense heat will slowly burn a hole into the wood. Our ancestors used wet sand along with the direction of airflow through the reed to control the shape and depth of the bowl. Coal-burned containers can be used for all kinds of water chores. To boil water in your container, add red-hot rocks from the fire.

PILLOWCASE WATER CARRY

It may be necessary in a survival scenario to carry large quantities of water (5+ gallons, which with water weighing around 8 pounds per gallon means carrying 40 pounds). Whether traveling in barren lands or hydrating a large group several hundred yards from a water source, you should know a few water-carrying techniques.

Line a pillowcase (burlap bags or feed sacks also work) with a thick plastic trash bag. You can then pour several gallons of water inside it. The cloth lining helps not only to stabilize the load but also to protect the lining from rips and tears during travel. To carry, fold it over the top and tie it closed to create a seal, then lash the top knot of this bag to the top knot of another equally full bag. These bags can now be safely and securely carried over your shoulder with much less effort than hauling water by hand in buckets.

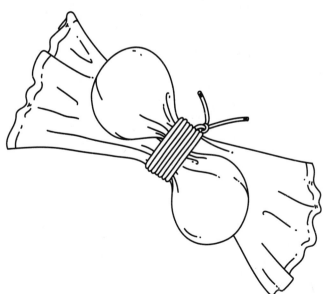

HAPPY BIRTHDAY CONTAINER

I'll never forget walking through the woods one day when I was a kid and seeing a cluster of shiny silver deflated helium birthday balloons hanging from a tree branch. After retrieving them with a stick I was surprised to find a note that had been written from a girl 3 states away and tied to the bottom before she released them on her birthday. It was like a modern-day note in a bottle. Since that time I've found deflated helium balloons in the wilderness on several occasions. Their Mylar surface can be used for a variety of purposes, including a reflective shelter back wall and even solar fire starting. They also make excellent water containers. Trim the filler neck off, fill with a liter or so of water, and tie on a spout similar to the one described in the Condom Canteen hack in this chapter. Voilà—instant bota bag.

MOUTH SPREADER CANTEEN BAIL

A pot handle, called a bail, makes hanging a pot over a fire very convenient. Many metal canteens don't come with bails and, consequently, are cumbersome when it comes to boiling and purifying wild water. An outstanding and little-known hack solution to this frustration can be found in the fishing department at almost any big-box outdoor retailer. A fish mouth spreader, when opened entirely, fits perfectly and securely inside the mouth of many different-sized metal canteens. This can be used to not only lift the vessel in and out of hot coals but also as a bail for hanging it above the fire when desired. This tool costs less than $2 and weighs virtually nothing. It is a great addition to any metal canteen water kit. This hack works especially well with Klean Kanteen brand containers.

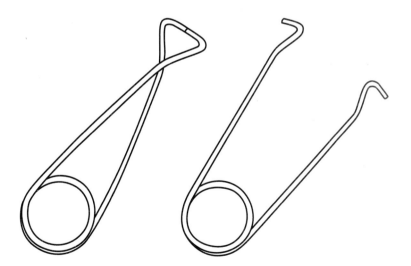

AN ALUMINUM FOIL CONTAINER THAT IS ACTUALLY USEFUL

Many people advocate packing aluminum foil into small everyday carry (EDC) survival kits. Often, you'll hear them say, "Aluminum foil can make a great container." In reality, this is easier said than done. It requires a bit of skill to shape a piece of aluminum foil into a usable container. It's something that most people don't think about until it's too late. This is a hack best taught by video. Click on the following link to watch as a few folds turn a square piece of aluminum foil into a very useful survival bowl that can be used to boil water, cook stews and broths, or even fry meat and vegetables. *www.youtube.com/watch?v=K2nC6T4muso.*

KILL IT WITH HOUSEHOLD BLEACH

Many cities purify their municipal water supply with chlorine. You can do the same in a survival scenario using household bleach. Most homes, businesses, and retail establishments keep a bottle of bleach on hand, and memorizing the purification dosages could keep you from a gastrointestinal nightmare. Household bleach is sold as a 6–8 percent concentration of active sodium hypochlorite. This is often marketed as *Extra Concentrated*. The Environmental Protection Agency (EPA) recommends using 2 drops of this concentration per 1 quart or liter of water. Make sure the water is clear to begin with and that you wait a full 30 minutes after adding the bleach before using it. Cloudy or murky water drastically affects the effectiveness of almost all chemical purifiers. Also, only use regular unscented bleach.

TRASH BOTTLE SOLAR DISTILLER

Distillation is the process of evaporating water and then condensing it again in a container. This process removes impurities, chemicals, salt, and even waterborne pathogens. All life raft survival kits include a solar distiller to desalinate salty ocean water in a survival scenario. You can easily hack a mini distiller from a clear trash bottle, such as a 2-liter bottle, in just a few minutes. Cut the bottom off the bottle and fold the bottom 2" of edge up under and inside the bottle. I've found it helpful to heat the bottom edge over a fire to make it more pliable. Place this bottle in a mud puddle, on wet sand, on a wet rag, or over a cup filled with dirty water and let the sun go to work. Clean, drinkable water will evaporate and condense on the inside of the bottle. It will then run down the inside of the bottle and collect in the folded lip that you created. Then it can be drunk from the bottle without further purification. *Note:* Full sun is required for the distillation process to work.

BOIL WATER IN A LARGE LEAF

Boiling is hands down the most effective primitive survival method of water purification. It effectively kills all viruses, protozoan cysts, and bacteria. However, a metal pot or canteen isn't always available in a survival scenario. Believe it or not, you can still boil water in plastic bottles, paper cups, and even leaves! To boil water in a leaf, shape it into a cup, place it into the coals of a fire, and quickly fill it with water. You have to fill it with water fast because it's only the water that prevents the leaf (or plastic and paper) from burning. This is possible because of conduction; the heat from the fire is conducted away from the leaf and into the water. The edge of the leaf may burn but the parts touching water will not. Primitive cultures have been boiling in leaf containers for centuries! *Hint*: Practice this at home using a large cabbage leaf.

SINK FILLER HACK

If you're on the move and have to fill up canteens or containers from public restrooms, you may find it difficult to fit them under the sink faucet for filling. One quick hack is to cut a small hole in the bottom side of an empty water bottle and place it under the faucet stream. The water will go into the bottle through the hole and then drain out the mouth, which can be directed over the sink lip into your container. A dustpan (cleaned first of course) can be used as a quick diverter as well. Allow the stream to fall onto the pan and it will flow through the gutter-like handle into your container.

DRINK WITH A BANDANA

Many people completely overlook one of the best sources of water in a survival scenario—*dew*. The dew that collects on grass, rocks, and leaves is 100 percent safe to drink without purification. The trick is collecting it. I've experimented with many ways and have found the best collection method is to mop it up with a bandana or T-shirt and wring it out every few mops into a container. I have collected more than 2 gallons of water in under 1 hour using this method in a small meadow near Willow Haven (my survival training facility). Grasses are not poisonous so there is no general risk with mopping dew from meadows, fields, or transition areas that lead into forests. If you're wearing clothing, then you have a means of collecting dew.

2-LITER RAIN COLLECTOR

The ability to collect rainwater, especially if stranded on an ocean island, is critical. Here's a great hack about how to turn plastic water bottles into powerhouse rain collectors. Start by cutting off the bottom of the bottle (be sure it has a cap to seal the mouth). Next, cut vertical slices down the side of the bottle about halfway down starting at the bottom. Make the slices 1"–2" apart. Fold the sections out, giving the bottle a flower-like appearance. Heating up this bend to make it more pliable speeds up the process and helps keep the petals in place. Finally, secure the cap of the bottle a couple inches in the ground and wait for rain. This is modeled after nature itself. The leaves on many plants and trees help funnel rainwater toward the main trunk. These plastic "petals" help to funnel rainwater into the central reservoir. The water can then be drunk with a straw or piece of hollow reed grass.

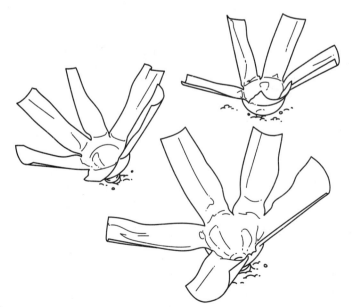

UMBRELLA WATER FUNNEL

Most people think of umbrellas as a tool to keep them dry. In this hack, we flip an umbrella's function on its head—literally! Rain is one of the best sources of survival water. It is one of the few natural sources of water that can be consumed without filtration or purification. Collecting it, however, can be a challenge with limited resources. Gathering rain is all about one critical detail: *surface area*. The larger your collection area, the more rain you will gather. You can create a very effective rain collector by flipping an umbrella upside down and placing it on top of a bucket. Then, poke a couple holes in the middle. Now, you've turned an umbrella into a giant funnel. In my tests, a 3'-diameter umbrella can harvest around 3 gallons of rainwater per 1" of rain. That's enough for 3 days for one person in a survival scenario!

MAKE A SOLAR WATER BLANKET

Water vapor evaporates from plant and tree leaves through a process called transpiration. It's very similar to perspiration for humans. This process is accelerated when a plant or leaf is covered in clear plastic sheeting in full sun. An easy way to gather transpired plant water is to lay a sheet of clear plastic on a patch of grass as if it were a blanket. There must be full sun or the process does not work. After a couple of hours the underside of the plastic will be covered in small droplets of drinkable water. Carefully turn over the plastic sheet and mop the water with a bandana or T-shirt and wring it directly into your mouth or a container for travel.

Chapter 3

Fire Hacks

**MAKING THE MOST OF MATCHES AND
DISPOSABLE LIGHTERS HACKS**

IGNITION HACKS

F ire is directly related to every other survival priority. It helps regulate core body temperature as well as makes up for a lack of proper sheltering knowledge or materials. It can boil and purify water, cook food, signal for rescue, and even help make tools such as containers and spears.

Knowing how to light a fire is one of the survival skills that takes the most practice to understand and master. There is a lot to learn, including basic principles about tinder properties, ignition tools and strategies, friction dos and don'ts, fuel types, carrying methods, and more. Fire is also the survival category that allows for the most creative hacking, which is why I love it so much. Creating fire is without question my favorite survival skill to practice and teach. The number of hacks in this chapter is not only influenced by the previous two statements but also by the importance of fire in general.

This chapter is the culmination of almost 20 years of fire hacking. In it we'll explore some of the craziest and unique ways of making fire using random, everyday objects you've ever seen. Enjoy!

MAKE "*THE BEAST*" MATCH

When I was a kid, the dad of a friend of mine used to make slow-burning fuses for our model rockets out of cotton yarn and match heads. He would take a box of wooden matches, pinch off the match heads, and crush them up to a fine powder using a mortar and pestle. Then he would add some water to the powder and make a paste into which he would dip the cotton thread and let dry. When lit, it would burn like a slow fuse. You can make your own beast match in a similar way.

Grind up the match heads from a bunch of wooden matches to a fine powder and mix in some water to make a paste. Then take small matchsticks made from split fatwood (resin-rich pinewood) and dollop a big glob of match-head paste about ¼" around by 1" long onto the end and let dry for at least a day. You can strike these just like regular matches, except now you have a beast match.

A PERFECTLY MINTY LIGHTER BOX

As convenient as disposable cigarette lighters are for starting fires, they certainly have drawbacks. First, if the fuel lever is accidentally depressed in your pack, it's very possible your lighter can empty itself during travel. Second, disposable lighters do not work well (or sometimes not at all) when wet. One quick dunk in a river or pond could mean no chance of success. Lastly, at very cold temperatures, disposable lighters are very unreliable because the butane fuel is less likely to vaporize. One simple hack for protecting (and even insulating) your disposable lighter is to pack it inside a Mentos brand gum container. This container makes a perfect little lighter box because it's water-resistant and also protects the fuel lever from being depressed. There is also just enough extra space for some good fire tinder like steel wool or cotton balls. This makes a perfect mini hack survival kit container, which I've featured in Chapter 8 of this book.

CARDBOARD TRIPLE THREAT

Corrugated cardboard has small channels that fit wooden matches perfectly when it's cut to the right size. Cut a piece of cardboard with 3 vertical channels just long enough to fit wooden strike-anywhere matches. Dip this entire triple-threat match in melted wax 3 times to waterproof the cardboard and the match heads. When ready to use, scratch the wax off the match heads and strike on a rock or other abrasive surface. One match will light the other 2, which will then light the cardboard. This is a great hack to make a match that is not only waterproof but also a very good fire starter. The cardboard will burn like a candle wick and will be very difficult to extinguish even in light drizzle and heavy wind.

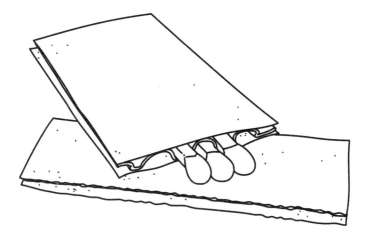

P, B, & F(IRE)

Jars of all shapes and sizes, such as peanut butter and jelly containers, make awesome waterproof fire kits. Make a P, B, & F(ire) jar by packing an empty jar with strike-anywhere matches and cotton balls. I prefer plastic jars because they're more durable. Just in case you don't have a suitable striking surface, glue a circle of 220-grit sandpaper to the inside of the jar lid.

Bonus hack: Mix your cotton balls with petroleum jelly for a fire starter that will burn 100 times as long as a regular cotton ball. Prevent a mess by packing these inside a resealable bag before putting them in your fire jar. With this prepared kit, you now have a grab-and-go fire jar with everything you need to get a fire going—*fast!*

SALVATION FOR WET MATCHES

Even wet matches can be saved if you know how. Many outdoorsmen and outdoorswomen travel in cold-weather climates with HotHands Hand Warmers. These air-activated warmers not only can be used to warm and ready hands for fire making, but they can also dry out wet matches. Place wet matches along with 1 or 2 activated HotHands warmers into any dry pocket and wait at least 45 minutes. The dry, radiant heat from the warmers should dry the matches out enough to allow ignition. Don't give up if your first attempt at striking isn't successful. Very wet matches may take longer to dry, but you can do it!

MATCH FEATHER STICK

If you've studied survival or bushcraft very long, chances are you've heard of "feather sticks." With a sharp knife, shave long wood slivers down the side of a stick. Just before the sliver is shaved off, stop and begin another sliver from the top. After several minutes' work, you'll have a stick covered in feather-like wood shavings. These shavings catch fire much quicker and easier than the larger solid stick. Consequently, feather sticks are an excellent fire-starting hack. However, let's take that concept a step further and apply it to wooden matches. In extremely difficult conditions when you might need additional help starting a fire, use your knife to shave small wooden slivers just above the match head, creating a mini feather stick. When the match ignites it will very quickly catch these shavings on fire, which will create a stronger and bigger flame.

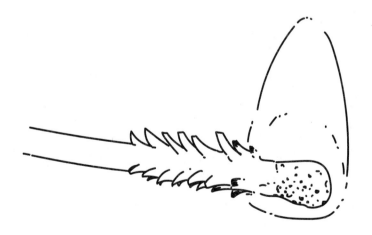

COTTON FIRE CIGAR

This is a friction fire start that will blow your mind. Start by pulling apart cotton balls (or tampons) and flatten the pieces onto a board so that you make a flat rectangle about 3" × 8". Sprinkle a line of wood ash about the size a pencil along one end. Next, roll the ash up inside of the cotton like a cigar. Continue to pack and roll it with your hands so that it's fairly compacted. Finally, place the cotton/ash cigar between 2 boards and move the top board back and forth so that the cotton/ash cigar rolls beneath it on the other board. Continue to do this very fast with medium pressure for about 1 minute. The friction of the carbon particles in the ash combined with the pressure will cause a small ember to form in the cotton fibers. The cotton can be pulled apart, and you can blow the ember into flame!

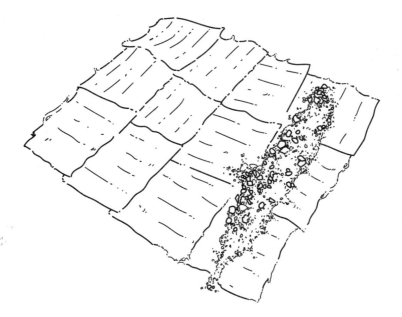

MAKE A STRIKING SURFACE

If no striking surface is available for a wooden match, hack your own with a little bit of sweat equity. You'll need 2 dry pieces of wood to get the job done. With your match at the ready, rub 1 piece of wood against the other until it gets very hot and starts to smoke and char a little bit. When it does this, strike your wooden match on that hot surface. The heat from the friction will be enough to ignite the volatile phosphorus on the head of the match. This method works better if you carve the piece of wood you're rubbing with into a chisel shape and push it back and forth across the other dry stick. This method takes a little effort but may be the missing link you need to get a fire going!

JUMPER CABLE + PENCIL = FIRE

Using a battery power source is a very popular fire-starting method. There are many different ways to do it using many different power sources. This one involves using a car battery, jumper cables, and a regular No. 2 pencil.

Start by shaving down an area on each end of the pencil about as wide as the jumper cable alligator clamps. Make sure that the pencil lead is exposed. Then clamp on the positive and negative jumper cable clamps, one on each shaved area. Be sure the clamps are touching the pencil lead. Place the clamps and pencil on top of your tinder bundle and turn on the car engine. The electricity from the cables will turn the pencil lead into a red-hot ember and the wooden pencil will erupt into flame in about 2 minutes' time. Use the flame to ignite your tinder bundle.

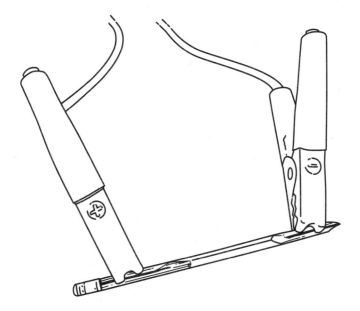

MAKE FIRE FROM A *BUSTED* CIGARETTE LIGHTER

I've found discarded cigarette lighters in the most unlikely places: on the side of the road, on hiking trails, washed up on beaches, and even in a cave. Although they are almost out of fuel or busted altogether, you can still use them to start a fire if you know how. A broken or empty lighter will produce a spark, and that spark can be used to ignite tinder.

One of my favorite tricks is to use a broken lighter to ignite a Q-Tips ear cleaner. Fuzz up the cotton tip by pulling at the cotton fiber, and strike the lighter into the fibers. The same can be done with cotton bandages, cotton balls, dryer lint, and even the dried seedheads from many grasses, cattail, and milkweed. See the Make Your Own Lint for Tinder hack later in this chapter for how to make your own lint in a survival scenario.

3 BOW-DRILL BEARING-BLOCK HACKS

There are many factors to consider when building and successfully using a bow-drill friction fire set. From available wood types to cordage resources, there are many variables that you must control. You can greatly increase the chances of a fast ember by maximizing friction between the bottom portion of the spindle and hearth board and minimizing it at the top between the spindle and the bearing block. Three low-friction bearing-block hacks you can try include a skateboard wheel (the bearing in the middle provides nearly frictionless spinning), a shot glass, and a penny that has been pounded into a concave shape using a ball-peen hammer or metal punch (glue this into a depression carved into a wooden handhold).

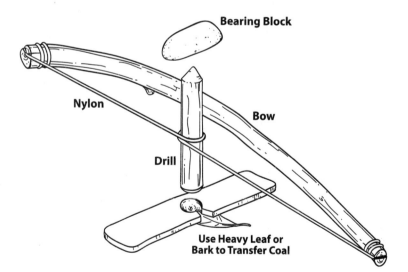

Bearing Block

Nylon

Bow

Drill

Use Heavy Leaf or Bark to Transfer Coal

9-VOLT RAZOR HACK

Batteries, as I said before, can be used in all kinds of different ways to make fire. For instance, you can use a 9-volt battery and grade #0000 steel wool. Steel wool will ignite when it's connected to the positive and negative terminals of a 9-volt battery. Similarly, you can use the very thin blades from a disposable razor to short-circuit a 9-volt battery. A tiny spark will fly when a blade touching the positive terminal is crossed with a blade touching the negative terminal. The correct tinder at this intersection, such as char cloth or thin shreds of tinder fungus, can be ignited with little effort. The metal or wire used to short-circuit a low-voltage battery such as the one you're using for this hack must be extremely thin in order to deliver positive results. *Note:* Keep in mind that repeated attempts can drain the charge from your battery source.

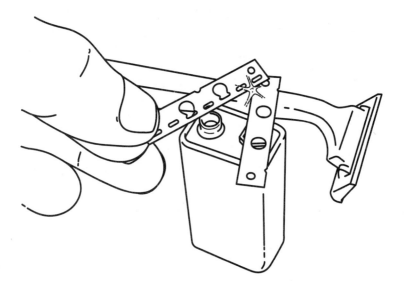

ANTENNA BELLOWS

A bellows is any device used to blow oxygen into a fire to increase the rate of combustion. The more oxygen a fire gets, the stronger and hotter it will burn. This is why blowing on a fire helps keep it going. The ability to concentrate this stream of oxygen into the heart of a fire can grow it exponentially.

One great bellows hack is a car or radio antenna—or rather the metal housing that protects the antenna wire. Whether retractable or of a fixed length, these metal casings are hollow and make an excellent fire-resistant, lightweight bellows. Simply place one end of the antenna into the heart of a struggling fire and blow through the other end to inject much-needed oxygen. The retractable antenna from an old radio makes a great compact addition to any fire kit!

GIVE YOUR BOW DRILL MORE ENERGY

As I said earlier, when building a bow-drill kit, you want to reduce the amount of friction in the handhold portion of the spindle and increase it at the hearth board. I've seen many different attempts to reduce friction at the bearing block that sits on top of the spindle, including oil, green leaves, and even a mechanical bearing. In a pinch, you can hack a mini energy drink bottle into a low-friction bearing block. Cut the bottom from the bottle. Place it over a spindle, holding it hammer-grip style to apply pressure. The top of the spindle must be carved larger than normal and more rounded on top so that it does not drive into the cap portion of the bottle. A round, bulbous top on the spindle will allow it to spin with incredibly low friction while nested within the top walls of the bottle.

LIGHT YOUR FIRE WITH A LIGHT BULB

A traditional incandescent household light bulb filled with water makes an incredible solar fire-starting lens (modern compact fluorescent energy-efficient bulbs will not work). It is the perfect spherical shape. However, there are some hacks to make it work! First, wrap the bulb in an old rag or T-shirt and gently tap the very bottom electrical contact point with a hammer or knife handle. After a few solid hits it will loosen and you can pull it out. Then gently break out the stem and filament, work it out through the hole, and discard it. The inside of most light bulbs are coated with silica. Rinse this out with water because you want to use a clear bulb. Now, turn the bulb upside down, fill it with clear water, and use it as an incredible solar lens. This is one of the most effective fire starters I've ever used.

POM PYRO

Trash water bottles can be found in every urban location and even in the most remote wilderness locations. With a little knowledge, these trash bottles can be filled with water and used as a solar magnifier to start a fire. My favorite bottle to use is the double-sphere POM juice bottle. When that bottle is filled with water I can smolder tinder in less than 3 seconds on a sunny day. Many bottles are effective fire starters. Place the bottle 1" from the tinder and then slowly pull back the bottle toward the sun until you see a wisp of smoke. My 6 favorite solar tinders are chaga (tinder fungus), char cloth, milkweed ovum, charcoal, rabbit/deer poop, and punky wood (soft, rotting wood usually from the center of a tree or log—see the Rotten Wood = Fire Gold hack later in this chapter for more on punky wood).

FIRE FROM ICE

If you can use water to make fire, then can you use ice? Of course you can. The trick is carving a chunk of ice into a perfect sphere for magnifying the sun's rays. This is where the hack comes into play. Start by sawing a rough globe from a chunk of ice. I've found this is much easier with a saw than carving it with a knife. Then use the mouth of your water bottle as a shaving tool (metal bottles work best). If you press the mouth of the bottle against the roughly shaped ice ball and begin to work it round and round, it will eventually turn the ice into a perfect circle. The circular shape of the bottle mouth makes the ice ball into a sphere. Use this clear sphere to focus the sun's rays on tinder.

A MYLAR EMERGENCY SURVIVAL BLANKET LENS

You can start a solar fire with the sun's rays using a Mylar blanket, a container with a plastic snap-on lip, and a hollow tube or ink pen. First, trim out the inside of the plastic lid so that it is just the rim that snaps onto the container. This circular rim will tightly hold a piece of Mylar placed over the top. Pierce a hole in the side of the container and insert a hollow tube or ink pen. This allows you to suck the sealed Mylar into a convex parabolic shape that can create a solar ember in direct sunlight on suitable tinders such as punky wood, agave pith, deer poo, char cloth, and tinder fungus (chaga).

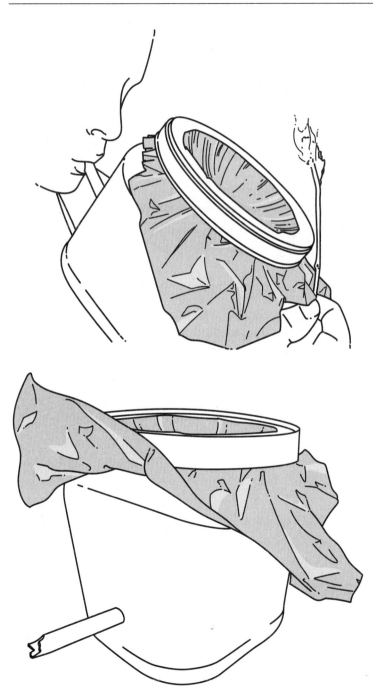

MAKE A FIRE PIPE

Many small snack cups and coffee containers are sealed with a Mylar covering. Although you may be tempted to gobble down these snacks in a survival scenario, before you break the Mylar seal use a package like this as a solar fire-starting tool. By inserting a hollow tube, section of bamboo, or ink pen through the side of the snack cup, you can suck and draw the reflective Mylar seal inward to form a parabolic lens. A parabolic, or convex, lens works to converge the sun's rays to a focal point that can be used to generate a smoldering ember. Rubber grip pens work very well because they create a better seal when inserted through the plastic wall of the container. Great solar ember tinders are chaga, char cloth, deer or rabbit poop, punky wood, the tea from inside tea bags, and dried ground coffee.

BAD EYES = GOOD FIRE

In the eyeglass section at almost any pharmacy store you will find a display of credit-card-sized magnifying glasses intended to aid reading by those with poor eyesight. To the well-informed student of survival, this small lens is one of the best fire starters available. This inexpensive wallet-sized magnifier can create an ember on punky wood, char cloth, dry deer poop, tinder fungus, sage, and a variety of dried leaves in just a few seconds on a bright sunny day. I always have one in my wallet, and I consider it one of the most reliable fire starters I've ever used. In fact, here is a video I filmed to explain exactly how to use it for fire starting: *www.willowhavenoutdoor.com/punky-wood-video*.

FROM FLASHLIGHT TO FLAME

The convex reflector that surrounds the bulb of a flashlight reflects the light from the bulb into a strong and focused beam. If removed from the case, it can also be positioned to create a solar ember on tinder held in the proper position. First, remove the reflector from the flashlight case. This often requires removing the bulb and plastic/glass lens cover. Stab your small piece of solar tinder onto the end of a thin stick or wire and feed it up through the hole in the bottom of the reflector. Face the reflector directly into the sun and carefully position the tinder so that it rests in the spot with the tightest focal point of converged sunlight. Once it ignites, place it into a tinder bundle and blow it into flame. Best tinders are char cloth, deer or rabbit poo, chaga fungus, punky wood, milkweed ovum, and charcoal. *Note*: The reflectors in vehicle headlights also work very well for this.

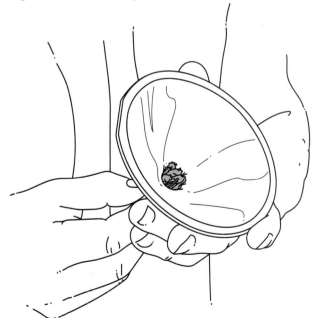

ROMANTIC HOUSE FIRE

I'll never forget a news clip I saw years ago about how a homeowner poured a glass of white wine, relaxed in her chair, and fell asleep only to wake up and find her house on fire. How did it happen? She placed her glass of white wine (nearly clear in color) on the coffee table next to the chair and right by the window. The sun was shining brightly through the window that day, and the circular shape of her wine glass converged the sun's rays to focus on a box of tissues sitting nearby. The focal point was so hot that the tissues caught fire, and the rest is history. As survivalists, we can learn a lot from this mistake. A clear bulbous sphere-like vessel filled with water (or any clear liquid) can be used to establish a solar ember when positioned properly.

PET BALLS

I'm going to start this hack section with one of the best (and most popular) fire hacks in the business—PET balls. These are cotton balls mixed with petroleum jelly; one of these will burn upward of 100 times longer than the same cotton ball without petroleum. The cotton ball behaves as a wick that burns the petroleum jelly fuel.

Many products are petroleum jelly–based, including some hair pomades, lip balms, first-aid ointments, and makeups. Any can be used. A PET ball that has been pulled apart to expose the tiny cotton fibers can ignite with just the small spark from a broken lighter or ferrocerium rod. A ferrocerium rod is a manmade metal that produces hot sparks when scraped against a sharp surface. To make mixing easier, I prefer to microwave the jar of petroleum jelly for a few seconds to liquefy it. I then pour it over a bowl of cotton balls.

THE FIRE PICK

Did you know that guitar picks make incredible fire
tinder? They are made from a material called celluloid,
which happens to be extremely flammable. For this reason
I always keep a couple in my wallet as emergency fire-
starting tinder. They will ignite when exposed to an open
flame such as that from a disposable lighter or match.
However, you can also use them with just a spark if you
know how. Start by drilling a small divot in a stick. Then,
split the stick in the end all the way into the divot. Next,
using your knife, fill the divot with shavings from the
guitar pick. Make these by scraping your knife at a
90-degree angle against the pick. Finally, slide the pick
into the split until the edge of it is buried in the shaving-
filled divot. Now you can ignite the small shavings using a
spark from the ferro rod, and they will in turn ignite the
pick. Voilà—fire with a guitar pick!

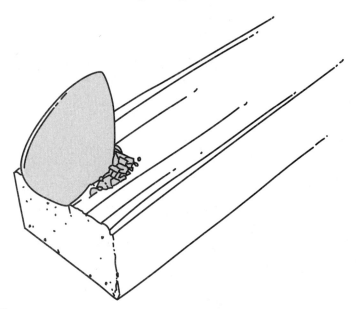

MAKE TINDER FROM A BUSTED LIGHTER

As you learned previously in the Ignition Hacks section, even a busted lighter can be used to ignite cotton fibers and dried seed pods. Did you know you can also make an incredible tinder from a broken lighter? Each time you turn the wheel against the lighter's mini ferro rod, it scrapes off a small amount of metal dust. This ferrocerium dust is extremely flammable. With the lighter turned upside down, turn the lighter wheel slowly about 50 times over a napkin and watch as the dust slowly collects in a little pile. Then, spark the lighter wheel into that dust pile for a short burst of flame. The small flame will ignite the napkin.

USE A POP CAN TO PLAN FOR FUTURE FIRES

Planning for future fires is a big part of survival. One of the best ways to do this is to make char cloth. It is a natural-fiber fabric (such as a 100 percent cotton bandana) that has been burned in the absence of oxygen. Cut an empty pop can in half, place several squares of natural-fiber fabric inside, and then pressure fit the top half over the bottom half. Next, close the thin metal seal to the drinking hole so that there is just a sliver of opening. Finally, place this container in the coals or a small fire for several minutes. You will see smoke and flames shoot out of the slit at the mouth hole. When the smoke stops your char cloth is done. After cooling, ignite it with a spark or lens, and place it in a tinder bundle to be blown into flame.

GUM WRAPPER FIRE

A foil-backed gum wrapper (or any foil-backed paper candy wrapper) can be used to start a fire if you have a battery source such as a AA battery from a flashlight or remote control. Start by trimming the wrapper to an hourglass shape. Touch the positive and negative terminals of the battery with the foil side of the wrapper simultaneously. The electrical current will converge on the thinnest part of the hourglass shape and ignite the wrapper to flame. If the battery is too weak to bring the wrapper to flame, consider adding a second battery for more electrical current. Be sure to have a good tinder bundle ready because you'll only have about 3 seconds of flame!

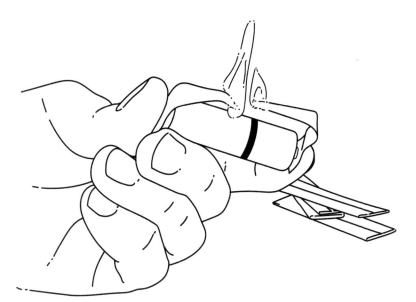

MAKEUP AISLE TO FIRE TINDER

Many female readers will be familiar with the flat, round cotton pads sold as makeup removers. These also happen to be one of my favorite ingredients in a fantastic do-it-yourself fire tinder. I call them fire discs. When candles in my house burn down to nothing I toss them in an old shoe box to repurpose. When I gather enough, I melt them down in an old saucepan until they are liquid. Then I fill that saucepan up with the flat cotton makeup removal pads and wait until they are saturated through with wax. Using tongs, I place them one by one on a board to cool and harden. These can be packed into old candy tins or resealable bags and make for one of the best fire starters I've ever used. Pull apart to expose the tiny cotton fiber and light with a spark or flame. Burn time: 5–10 minutes.

WALLET-SIZED FIRE SQUARES

I had a friend in college who needed to give himself regular injections of medicine. Each time he would reach into his desk drawer and pull out a little foil packet that contained a 1" × 1" square alcohol prep pad, which he'd use to disinfect the injection site before and afterward. I remembered this many years later when prepping for a survival-kit-building course. I needed a small, reliable fire tinder to pack into tiny candy-tin survival kits, and the alcohol prep pads were just the ticket. They work so well in fact that I keep a couple in my wallet just in case. They don't burn long, but they will give you an open flame with just a spark; you can use them to ignite a tinder bundle. You can purchase boxes of 100 at any pharmacy for under $5.

MAKE YOUR OWN LINT FOR TINDER

Most people know that dryer lint makes awesome fire tinder. It's dry, fibrous, and almost always contains cotton fibers, which are incredibly flammable. However, there are no dryer lint trees in the wilderness, or at least none that I've found. If you have an ignition source that will create a spark, such as a busted cigarette lighter or a ferro rod, here is a little trick to make your own lint tinder. Scrape any cotton garment at a 90-degree angle with a knife or sharp tool (even rock). You will slowly reveal a small pile of cotton fibers. Collect enough of them to create a tinder bundle large enough to ignite with just a spark. *Note:* Don't pack your lint too tight when trying to ignite it. Pull the fibers apart to expose more surface area and you'll increase the chances that a spark will take hold.

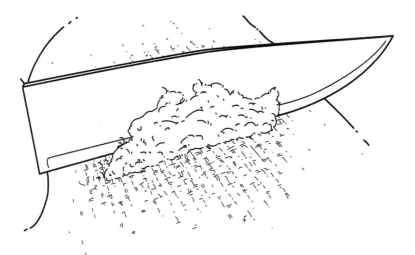

AMP UP YOUR SOLAR FIRE STARTING WITH CAFFEINE

There are very few items that will smolder like you need them to when starting a fire by magnifying the sun's rays. Dried coffee grounds and tea bags just happen to work. The key is that they must be *dry*. Once an ember has started to smolder using a solar lens, begin to make slow, steady circles with your focal point around that ember. This will grow and strengthen your ember into something that can then be transferred into a prepared tinder bundle. Dried tea or coffee won't burst into flame on their own. The resulting embers must blown in a tinder bundle to create flame.

WINDPROOF CANDLES

If you've ever struck a match only to have it blown out by a rogue gust of wind, then you will appreciate this hack. Several years ago I was at a birthday party for the son of a friend of mine. The cake was delivered with much anticipation and topped with 10 brightly burning birthday candles. I'll never forget the look on his face when the candles magically relit themselves just seconds after he thought his birthday wishes were sure to come true. On my way home that day I stopped by the local grocery store and picked up some relighting birthday candles. They make a great addition to fire kits and can be your best friend in the field when trying to start fires in inclement weather. As you saw in the Clothing Hacks and Footwear Hacks sections in Chapter 1, wax is also a great seam waterproofer.

ROTTEN WOOD = FIRE GOLD

Who would've ever thought that old rotting wood could save your life? Dry, rotting wood, called punky wood, is one of my all-time favorite survival fire-starting resources. It is the perfect medium for solar embers. Often, when starting fire using a solar lens you have to first develop a smoldering ember, then place that ember into a tinder bundle and blow it into flame. Punky wood makes a great ember that is not only self-sustaining but can easily be grown by crushing and sprinkling on more punk. The consistency of punky wood that you're looking for is dry, rotting wood that can easily be crushed and powdered between your fingertips. This wood can often be found in the form of dead branches on the forest floor, inside of hollow rotting trees, or on old, dry stumps. *Bonus tip*: You can also grow a bow-drill ember using powdered punky wood.

MOOSE POOP COULD SAVE YOUR LIFE

Another solar fire tinder hack is poop! I know, it sounds crazy but it's true. The dry vegetable matter–based poop from deer, moose, rabbits, goats, and cows makes excellent solar fire ember material. It smolders very well and is self-sustaining. I've found it best to pulverize it into a little pile on a dry wood shaving, a piece of bark, or right in the middle of your tinder bundle. Dry poop pellets from deer, rabbits, and moose also travel and store very well. They can be collected along the trail and kept in a container to use for future fires. If they are fresh, place them next to an existing fire to dry out or let them sit in full sun on a dark-colored rock. The rock will absorb the heat from the sun and help them dry from beneath.

WHEN YOUR ZIPPO GOES BLIPPO

Disposable cigarette lighters aren't the only ones that are still useful even when empty. Here's a Zippo lighter hack to keep in your back pocket just in case. Many people don't know that the fuel chamber of a Zippo lighter is packed with cotton batting. As I said in the PET Balls hack earlier in this chapter, cotton balls mixed with petroleum jelly is one of the most effective fire-starting tinders I have ever used in my life. The fuel-infused cotton batting inside a Zippo is very similar. You can easily pull it from the chamber, process it into a small fibrous tinder bundle, and then bring it to flame with the spark from the lighter's sparking wheel. An empty Zippo may not have fuel, but it certainly has tinder and can make fire!

SAVED BY THE Q-TIPS

As I said earlier, cotton balls mixed with petroleum jelly make some of the best fire starters on earth. If you didn't know this before, now you do! Sometimes in survival you have to think *outside* the box, and that often includes looking at everyday objects in a different way. Q-Tips, small cardboard sticks tipped with cotton, are a prime example of this. Even though it's not much cotton, it's enough to get a fire going in a pinch. It will also burst into flame with just a small spark, such as that from a ferro rod or broken lighter. The trick is to pull the cotton fibers apart and make a wispy tuft of cotton on the end of the stick. This creates more surface area for the spark to latch onto and almost guarantees you an open flame.

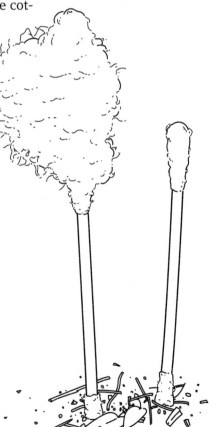

SNACK FOOD COULD SAVE YOUR LIFE

You've been told your entire life that snack food will kill you. What if I told you it could save your life—and it has nothing to do with eating? When it comes to fire, snack chips are some of the best kindling I've ever used. Many snack chips are fried in cooking oil, which happens to be very flammable. In damp or moist conditions when tinder is scarce, rip open a bag of oily chips and light them on fire. You'll have to use an open flame such as a lighter or match to get them going, but once ablaze they will burn long and strong even in inclement weather. Snack chips are also conveniently packed in waterproof packaging. *Note*: The inside shiny Mylar lining of most snack-food bags also has several survival functions, as you'll find in other hacks throughout this book.

FIRE FEATHERS

Your feather down–filled sleeping bag, vest, or jacket may be able to keep you warm in more ways than one in a cold-weather survival situation. Feathers (especially the light, fluffy, downy ones) make impressive fire tinder. The silver lining is that many down jackets and sleeping bag shells are water-resistant, which helps to keep the feathers dry inside. A handful of dry down feathers will ignite into flame with just a spark from a ferro rod or broken lighter. *Warning*: Feathers are what I call a *flash tinder*. This means they burn up in a flash and provide a survivor with little time to react. Be sure to have a good tinder bundle prepared before igniting your feather tinder.

TINDER PARMIGIANO

Have you ever been to a fancy Italian restaurant where the
waiter/waitress offers to grate fresh Parmigiano-Reggiano
cheese on your piping-hot dish of pasta? Believe it or not,
that cheese grater they are using is also really good at pro-
ducing fire tinder from dry wood. Softwood shavings from
trees such as willow, cottonwood, and tulip poplar make
excellent fire tinder for the beginning stages of a fire, just
after your tinder bundle catches to flame. A steel cheese
grater can make a quick pile of tinder shavings that's very
similar in effectiveness to a traditional feather stick. The
best use of this tool isn't in the field but rather in advance
when preparing for an adventure. I like to fill small reusable bags of fine wood shavings and throw a few in my
pack before I head out for an overnight camp. You never
know when dry wood tinder may be difficult to secure.

Chapter 4

Food Hacks

STOVE AND COOKING HACKS

FISHING HACKS

HUNTING AND FORAGING HACKS

In extreme conditions, humans can survive for as long as 3 weeks without food. While food may be on the bottom of the survival priority list, it can bring a survivor or group of survivors much joy. A meal in the wilderness not only provides needed calories and energy, but it can uplift spirits and boost morale. Just one meal may provide the hope necessary to make it through a difficult situation. Remember, survival is 90 percent mental and 10 percent physical. A full belly has just as much impact on attitude as it does on energy levels.

From cooking and preparation to hunting, fishing, and trapping, this chapter covers all kinds of incredible food- and eating-related hacks. These hacks may use random everyday objects, but they are based soundly on field- and time-tested survival principles. Many of the items used can be easily found or sourced in a sudden and unexpected survival scenario, often in the form of trash.

Securing food is usually the most time-consuming and difficult aspect of survival. Trying to outsmart animals while using improvised tools is not easy. Having a vast arsenal of options is a huge bonus. I hope this chapter provides you with a few more options to add to your existing list.

RAMEN NOODLE STOVE

I love items that do double duty. Ramen noodles are not only a lightweight pack food, but they can also serve as a great little cooking stove in a pinch. All you have to do is saturate the dried brick of ramen with a flammable liquid such as alcohol or HEET brand gas-line antifreeze (yellow bottle) and it will burn like a solid fuel puck for up to 20 minutes per side. The dried ramen noodles help to control the rate of fuel vaporization. It helps to soak the ramen brick in one of the fuels mentioned above for a while before use, but it isn't necessary. Build a makeshift frame to balance a pot and cook away! *Hint*: A standard yellow kitchen sponge also works the same way and makes a handy little impromptu stove when soaked with alcohol or HEET.

CARDBOARD FIRE ROLL

If you're looking for a quick and dirty way to cook a meal using a pan or skillet, the cardboard fire roll could be just what you need to get the job done. Roll pieces of cardboard into a tight log-like shape that is approximately 2' × 8' in diameter. Twist scrap wire around the cardboard log in 2 places to hold it together (old clothing hangers work great for this). Stand the roll upright atop 2 bricks spaced 6" apart so that air can draw through the hole up the center of the rolled log. Stuff the bottom interior of the roll with dry, combustible tinder such as leaves, grasses, newspaper, wood shavings, and twigs. Once ignited, the cardboard will continue to burn like a rocket stove until gone.

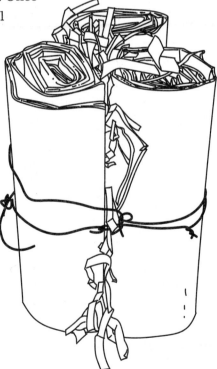

BRICK STACK COOKING SPIT

Two stacks of bricks, each on opposite sides of the fire, make an excellent frame for a cooking spit. Stack the bricks directly on one another with the holes aligned up and down. Once stacked to your preferred cooking height, insert 2 sticks into the holes of each stack of bricks. These sticks create a frame on top of each stack of bricks where a rotating cooking spit can be securely placed. Skewer your meat or vegetables on the spit and lay across the bricks in between the 2 stick guides on each stack. This stacked-brick technique works really well on extremely hard surfaces (like concrete) where forked supports cannot be hammered into the dirt. In cold weather, you can place the fire-heated bricks inside a shelter or under a raised bed to radiate heat throughout the night.

WOK SOLAR COOKER

A wok can be used to cook food in more ways than one if you understand how to harness the power of the sun. A wok, unlike most other pots and pans, has a consistent parabolic shape. When covered in a reflective material, this parabolic shape can be used to focus the sun's rays. A television satellite dish works in much the same way to converge electromagnetic signals into a receiver. You can use reflective aluminum tape, available at most hardware stores, to cover the wok's surface. Aim it at the sun and position it so as to cast a very hot focal point of light on a hanging pot or pan. The heat from this light will be enough to cook food and boil water. You can use this same setup to start a fire by placing tinder material at the focal point of light.

SATELLITE SOLAR COOKER

Small parabolic satellite dishes can be found anywhere there are houses. Their shape enables them to converge and concentrate the television signal into a receiver. They are also perfect tools for converging and concentrating the sun's rays for solar cooking. The inside of the dish must be covered with a reflective material. Reflective aluminum tape, available at most hardware stores, works best. However, you can adhere a Mylar blanket to the surface if you coat the satellite with petroleum jelly, lard, butter, or something similar first. Be careful because the focal point produced from this lens is incredibly powerful and can cause third-degree burns on human skin in just a few seconds. When ready to cook, suspend a pot (with the bottom spray-painted black to absorb heat) directly in the focal point. The dish must be facing directly toward the sun.

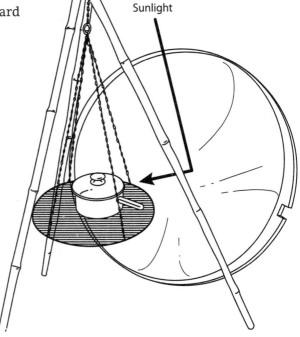

Sunlight

POP CAN ALCOHOL STOVE

You can make a very efficient little cooking stove in just a few minutes from 2 aluminum pop cans. Cut the lower third from both cans and pressure fit them together to make a closed container. Then, using a knife or spike, poke 6 holes around the top rim spaced equally apart and then also 2 or 3 in the middle of the bowl. Pour in an ounce or so of fuel and light with a match for an even, steady burn. The best fuels to use are available at nearly every grocery store, hardware store, or gas station. The 3 I've had success with are rubbing alcohol, denatured alcohol, and HEET brand gas-line antifreeze (yellow bottle). Once your stove is lit you'll need to create a stand to suspend your cup or pot above the stove. A couple bricks work really well for this.

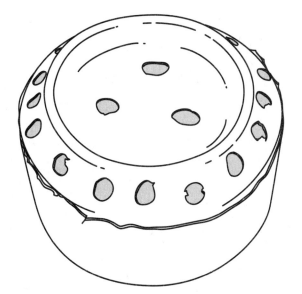

EGG CARTON BBQ

Starting charcoal briquettes can sometimes be a real challenge, and this little trick could make you the hero at your next family BBQ. Before heading out of the house, fill each space of an empty compressed paper (not Styrofoam) egg carton with a single charcoal briquette. About 15 minutes before you're ready to grill, light the 4 corners of the paper egg carton and watch as the paper burns and ignites the charcoal briquettes. This gives you a chance to reuse something that you'd normally throw away and also not have to use that nasty lighter fluid to get the BBQ going. *Bonus hack*: Paper egg cartons also make 12 great individual biodegradable seed starters.

TOILET PAPER STOVE

The ingredients list for this hack is simple: a can about the size of a roll of toilet paper (a 1-quart paint can works great), a roll of toilet paper, and a bottle of rubbing alcohol (denatured alcohol and HEET brand gas-line antifreeze also work). To start, crush the roll of toilet paper and cram it into the can. Next, slowly pour the bottle of rubbing alcohol into the can and let it completely saturate the toilet paper. To use the stove, ignite the top of the toilet paper with a match or lighter and you're ready to cook. When you notice the edges of the toilet paper are starting to burn, that means you are getting low on fuel. Snuff out the flame, add more alcohol, and relight. *Note*: If using indoors, be sure to crack a window because of carbon monoxide emissions.

TUNA CAN BURNER

Here's a cool little hack to not only heat your meal but also make a hot drink. You'll need a can of tuna packed in oil and a couple paper napkins. Remove the tuna lid and fold the napkins so they fit over the can opening with not much overlap except for the 4 corners. Give the oil a couple minutes to soak through the napkins. Once they are saturated with oil, light each corner on fire. The napkins will burn a surprisingly long time, creating a stove-like effect. The heat from the burning napkins will not only heat the tuna for a warm meal but can also be used to make a cup of hot tea in the process. Just build a couple supports on each side of the can to place a mug on and you'll be all set!

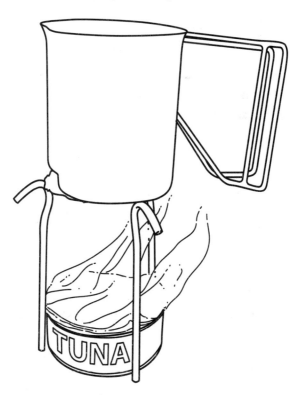

JUNK STOVE

You can make a very efficient little junk stove from an empty tuna can, some cardboard, and a variety of fuels. Cut 1" × 4" strips of cardboard and roll them into the empty can. Next, it's time to add fuel. Pour melted wax on top of the cardboard and light it; you can also use any kind of cooking oil to saturate the cardboard. The cardboard acts as a wick, and I've had junk stoves like this burn for as long as 30 minutes. What I love about this stove design is that it can be made from so many different "junk" pieces. Tin cans and cardboard are available almost anywhere.

NEWSPAPER OVEN

Believe it or not, you can cook fish in wet newspaper. After cleaning and gutting the fish, wrap it in 4 or 5 sheets of wet newspaper and place right into the coals of a fire. The fish will cook and steam inside, but the wet newspaper will not fail. The outer layer may scorch a bit, but the water prevents it from burning. Fifteen minutes should be sufficient to cook most fish as long as it is completely surrounded by coals. You can use paper grocery bags in place of newspaper. If you find it necessary to fry food on a sheet of aluminum foil in the coals of a fire, place sheets of wet newspaper underneath to help control the heat and prevent burning.

INVERTED CAN OVEN

One of my favorite hacked survival ovens is made with just an inverted metal can. In fact, when I'm lucky enough to trap, hunt, or catch a bird in the wild I will always try to cook it this way if the materials are available. After plucking, gutting, and dressing the bird, skewer it on a stake that has been driven straight into the ground. Next, place a metal can or container over the top of the bird and stake so that it covers them completely. Build a fire around the metal can and gather hot coals around it. A good coal bed will be necessary to cook the bird in a timely manner (typically 1 hour). I have also cooked fish using the same method; skewer the fish head down on the stake. Some of my finest wilderness meals have been cooked with this method. This is a very energy-efficient cooking method, allowing you to work on other camp chores while dinner is cooking.

IMPROVISED SWEDISH TORCH

This is a great hack to make a small-footprint wilderness cooking stove using just 3 sections of log. First, cut 3 24"-long lengths of seasoned wood. The diameter of each should be at least 6". Next, use your axe or knife to make cuts and chips all up one side of each of these logs. This exposes the wood inside, and the resulting slivers will more easily catch fire. Arrange the logs standing up in a triangle so that the chipped areas are all facing inward toward each other. There should be less than 2" of space between them. Finally, fill the center cavity with fire tin-

der such as pine needles, twigs, bark, and leaves. Only minutes after this tinder is ignited, the logs themselves will begin to burn like a rocket stove. Place a skillet on top and cook as if you were in front of a range at home!

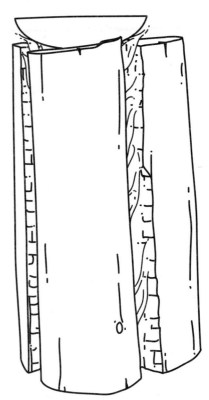

SHELF BRACKET STOVE

Being able to efficiently support or hang a cooking pot over a fire is sometimes easier said than done. One of my favorite quickie stove hacks involves 3 metal shelf brackets that cost under $5. They are also very lightweight and packable if you need to take them on the move. Once you've got a good bed of coals going, stab the metal L-shaped brackets into the ground as shown in the image and scoop the coals underneath. This makes for a very sturdy surface on which to cook stews, fry meats and wild veggies, or boil water. You can stab the short ends deeper in the ground to create a surface closer to the coals if necessary. Use 4 brackets to make a larger, square raised platform.

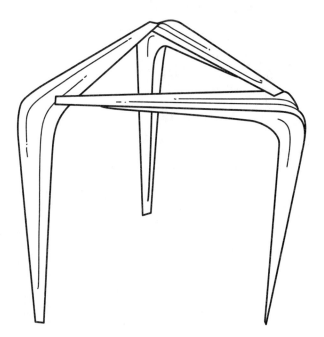

BRICK ROCKET STOVE

In a survival scenario you may need a stove for cooking that is both efficient (uses as little fuel as possible) and discreet (puts off little to no smoke). An improvised brick rocket stove is your answer to this need. To build one like that in the illustration you'll need to use 1 half brick for both the first and second layer. Layers 3, 4, and 5 will each use 4 full-sized bricks. A thin metal grill should be placed between layers 1 and 2 to keep the sticks and twigs off the ground and allow for maximum airflow. Stoves of this design burn at almost 100 percent efficiency and have very little leftover ash or smoke. The design shown requires 20 bricks, 2 of them split in half.

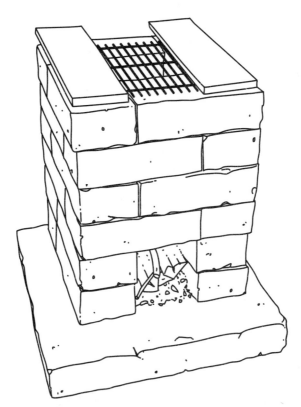

MAKE A WALKING OVEN

A very effective traveling stove for cooking fish and meats can be made from almost any tin can or metal container. First, pack the bottom 2"–3" of the stove with dry, punky (semi-rotted) wood. Next, add a layer of hot coals from the fire pit. Place your meat or fish (wrapped in aluminum foil, green nonpoisonous leaves, or wet newspaper) on top of the coals and cover it with another layer of coals. Finally, pile on another 2"–3"-thick layer of punky wood. The wood will allow the coals to smolder around the meat. Tie a rope or wire handle to the container for easy traveling. A small walking oven such as this one can cook fish in 15–20 minutes. Its obvious advantage is that you can carry it with you.

THE FISHERMAN'S BRACELET

Survival hacking sometimes involves preplanning. This is a simple and easy project that ensures you always have fishing tools. String and tie off 25' of fishing line between the eyelets of 2 fishing swivels so that the total length from swivel tip to swivel tip will wrap around your wrist. This forms a bracelet and the swivel clips act as the clasp.

I keep 3 different-sized fish hooks under the sole inserts of all my shoes. Making a usable hook in the wild is not easy, and they're not nearly as effective as modern hooks. Now, with a hook, line, and optional swivel, you have everything you need to effectively make a hack fishing pole and catch fish.

CREDIT CARD LURE

Let's face it, a credit card will do you little good in a survival scenario. Or will it? A rigid PVC credit card can be
hacked into several useful items. One of my favorites is a
fishing lure. You can cut a mini fish-shaped lure from a
credit card (or loyalty card or hotel key) with a knife or
pair of scissors. At the tail end of the minifish, carve 2
hook-shaped curls, one on top and one on bottom. Though
these little plastic hooks aren't as effective as their metal
counterparts, they are rigid enough to get a stubborn fish
to shore. Many credit cards are colorful and have small
reflective holograms, which help to get the attention of a
hungry fish. *Note*: The reflective holograms can also be
used as a signal mirror to reflect the sun's rays and flash a
signal to rescue crews.

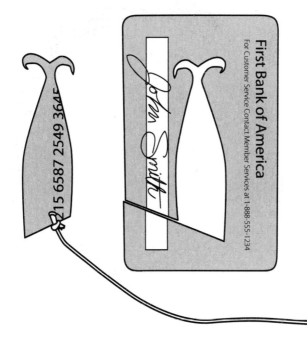

POP CAN FISHING KIT

Just when you think you've reached a location where no other human has been, you see a beer or soda can. Although it's not what you want to see on a pleasant day hike, in a survival scenario you can transform it into an effective hack fishing kit. The can itself makes a great tackle box for live bait. Just carve a wooden plug for the hole to keep the critters inside. Two simple cuts to the pop tab using your multitool make a very effective fishing hook—even with a little barb if you make your cuts wisely (notice how the cut section of the tab forms a small barb in the illustration). Scoring with your knife and then bend-breaking the pop tab will also work in a pinch if you don't have a multitool. Finally, the drinking hole seal flap makes a great flashy spoon lure to draw attention to your live bait. Punch a hole and thread it on your line just above the hook.

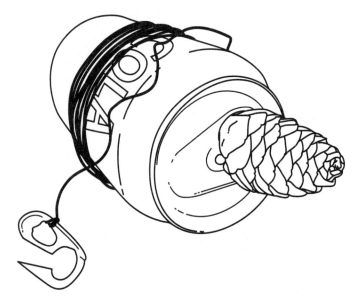

SPIDER WEB NET

During certain times of the year (typically spring and fall) the forest is filled with dew-soaked spider webs in the mornings. This is the perfect opportunity to make a spider web fishing net. Cut a 48" flexible green branch from any live tree. It should be less than ¼" in diameter. After trimming the leaves and branches, bend the top down to form an oval net frame. Tie it in place with a small piece of twine or bark cordage. Next, walk through the forest and sweep 20–30 spider webs onto the frame. As you sweep them up you will see the net grow stronger and stronger. Once it is strong enough to catch a small pebble it is ready to sweep through shallow pools and along the banks of ponds and streams to catch bait minnows and tadpoles. These can then be used to catch larger fish for cooking.

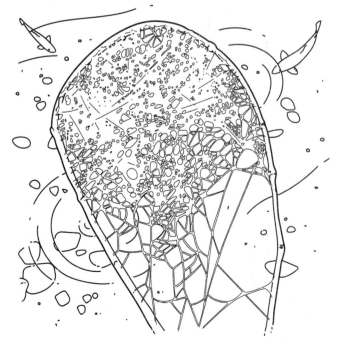

5-GALLON BUCKET AQUA LENS

Ponds, rivers, lakes, and streams can be a survival buffet of food. Wild edibles such as crayfish, clams, fish, turtles, and frogs can often be less than 2' beneath the water's surface but are difficult to see because of sun glare, ripples, or poor lighting. You can quickly make an incredible aqua lens to see almost perfectly beneath the water's surface. Cut the bottom from a 5-gallon bucket (or any bucket), tape a water-proof flashlight to the inside near the bottom, and plunge it into the water. The bucket provides a barrier that eliminates waves and ripples that disrupt your view, and the flashlight can light up the dark and shadowed areas.

PARACORD FISHING FLY

One of my students showed me this hack several years ago, and I've tested it time and time again in the fishing pond at Willow Haven. Slide a 1" section of paracord over a bare fishing hook to make a very appealing fishing fly lure. Fluff up the end over the hook for disguise and then heat the other end with an open flame to melt and weld it just below the eye where the line attaches. Live bait is always best, but when live bait isn't available you'll never miss an inch of paracord from your shoelaces or bracelet. This impro-vised fly lure also floats very well for top-water bluegill and bream fishing.

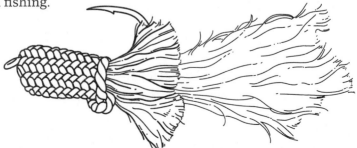

AN ENERGETIC FISHING HOOK

Making an improvised fishing hook from natural materials in the field can be very difficult. Hacking one from man-made materials is still hard but not impossible. To get either right, prepare for an exercise in patience. It's hard to manufacture a hook-shaped object that is rigid enough and sharp enough to hold a fish. You can carve one that meets these criteria from the bottom circular rim of a mini energy drink bottle. It's very strong and has a natural circular shape. Using a combination of cutting and abrading, fashion a strong, sharp hook. It isn't sharp enough to hold a fighting fish for long, but it will get the job done. Have your club or gig ready!

USE WALNUTS TO GET FISHING BAIT

My grandfather showed me this hack many moons ago, and it never ceases to amaze me and my students. Do the hack in fall when the walnuts are still wrapped in their green husks. I can guarantee you all the big red night-crawlers for fishing you'll ever need. Fill a 5-gallon bucket about half full of water. Then smash about 30 green walnuts with a rock and throw them one by one into the bucket of water. Next, stir this mixture vigorously for 5 minutes. Finally, clear the leaves and woodland duff from a 3' × 3' section of moist forest floor, and pour the rancid mixture evenly throughout. Like magic, red worms of all types and sizes will begin to writhe to the surface to escape the noxious poison. Green walnut husks have a high concentration of the compound juglone, which, in addition to annoying earthworms, can be used to paralyze fish in small pools.

PALLET BOW

Pallets can be used for more than just shelter (see the Pallet Shelter hack in Chapter 1). Believe it or not, one of the most incredible improvised bows I've ever used is made from just 1 pallet board. Start by removing one of the boards from the top of a shipping pallet. They are typically about 3" wide and about ½" thick. After removing the nails, either saw or split the board lengthwise. Taper the end of each length with your knife, one end being more tapered than the other. Carve 2 notches along the left and right edges of the less-tapered ends and lash them together, one board sandwiched on top of the other. Finally, carve your bow-string notches and string your bow for shooting. This hack is from my friends Hank Gevedon and Dave Mead of Reptile Toolworks and online at Kentucky River Trading Company (*www.kyrivertradingco.com*).

FIGURE-8 SLING BOW

I keep several climbing tools, including a climber's figure 8 and a couple of carabiners, in my bug out bag just in case I ever need them for rappelling over ledges, hoisting gear into trees, etc. What many people don't know is that a climber's figure-8 belay device doubles as an amazing sling bow with the simple addition of a set of high-power slingshot bands (which I also carry in my bug out bag). You can lash almost any set of bands, using dental floss or even zip ties, to either side of the large opening of the figure-8 device. Once done, the large open ring acts as an arrow guide for launching full-sized hunting arrows. It's easy and safe to use and is also very accurate. I use a 40-pound sling-shot band set, which is more than capable of taking almost any game animal in the Eastern Woodlands. Extra band sets can be found at *www.notifbutwhensurvivalstore.com*.

SPOON BROADHEAD

Whether you're hunting with bow and arrow or a spear, it's always better for it to be tipped with a sharp metal broadhead. Believe it or not, you can use something to kill your food that most people use to eat their food—a *spoon*! As you can see in this illustration series, the evolution of a regular spoon to a killer broadhead is a simple process. Pound the spoon flat with a rock or hammer. Next, file the edges down to a point, using a standard metal file that can be found in almost any auto repair shop or garage. Finally, snap off the handle at the base with repeated bending and lash the finished point into a split at the end of an arrow with dental floss. This hack is from my friends Hank Gevedon and Dave Mead of Reptile Toolworks and online at Kentucky River Trading Company (*www.kyrivertradingco.com*).

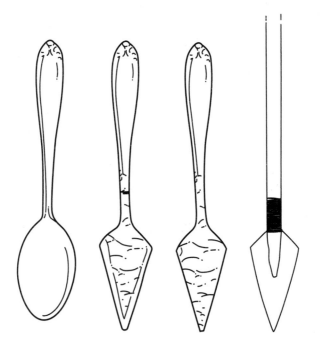

FROM TOY TO TAKEDOWN

One of my favorite childhood pastimes was battling with my brother, both of us running around in the woods, shooting each other with Nerf guns loaded with sponge-tipped darts. I recently picked one up for nostalgia and was surprised at the force with which the modern Nerf guns blast their ammo. In fact, the one I purchased shot at a velocity similar to the blowguns I use. After modifying an ammo round to give it a sharpened point, I could get it to stick in a tree from 10 yards away. In fact, I could create a grouping of arrows about the size of a dinner plate. This is a weapon capable of taking song birds in a survival scenario for small rotisserie meals. Clip off 2" lengths of a wire clothes hanger, sharpen one end by abrading it on concrete, and stab it in the end of a Nerf dart. Voilà—instant dart gun.

LOADS OF LARVAE

Most insects are edible. In fact, most people in the world eat insects. The big problem with insects is that you have to have a lot of them to make any kind of a caloric difference. Finding enough of them can be a huge challenge. However, if you stumble upon an ant hill, here's a hack that can score you loads of edible ant larvae. Ants' natural instinct is to protect their larvae from the sun and open air. They want to get them under cover as fast as possible. First, lay a tarp on the ground next to an ant mound and fold over one corner to create a protected area. Next, shovel ants and larvae from the mound on top of the tarp near the folded corner. The ants will carry the exposed larvae to any area of the tarp where an edge or corner is folded over to provide shelter. Let the ants work for a few minutes, then scoop the larvae out by the handful. They can then be fried or added to wilderness stews.

ORANGE SACK GHILLIE HOOD

As many hunters will tell you, good camouflage makes a big difference when trying to avoid being detected by wild game. The mesh bags that oranges come packaged in can be hacked to make a nearly perfect hood for a ghillie suit (a camouflage outfit that resembles heavy foliage). The base layer of most good ghillie suits is a mesh fabric in which different types of yarns, fibers, burlap strands, and natural materials are woven. This mix of materials not only creates an incredible break-up pattern, which breaks up the human outline so you aren't easily spotted, but it makes it easy to mix in natural vegetation from any location. Mesh orange bags can be used in a very similar way. Start by weaving earth-tone strands of yarn or strips of fabric in and out of the mesh to create a "wig-like" effect. Start with 12" strips that, when attached in the middle, create 2 6" strands. Complete the look by mixing in natural grasses from the environment.

BICYCLE-POWERED SLINGSHOT

A bicycle has everything you need to make a very powerful slingshot. Start by removing the front tire and fork from the bicycle. This fork turned upside down will serve as your slingshot fork. Next, remove the inner tube from the bicycle tire and cut 2 strips that are 15" × 1". These are your slingshot bands. Cut a 2" × 3" vinyl or leather patch from the bicycle seat and tie one end of each band to a hole you punch on each side of the patch. The best way to do this is to insert the band through the hole and lash it back on itself with twine. This will hold very well even under extreme pressure. Finally, lash the other end of each band to the metal fork and you're ready to launch anything from rocks and pebbles to pieces of scrap metal.

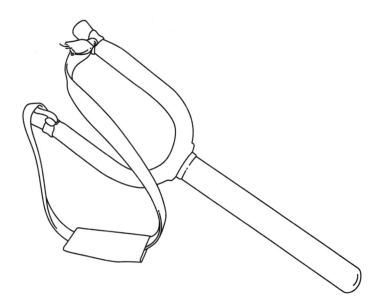

CROSS-COUNTRY TAKEDOWN BOW

I heard about a guy who used cross-country skis to make a takedown archery bow. His was complicated, with quite a bit of wood needed for the central wood riser. With some experimentation, I found that you can make a very powerful takedown bow from just a single pair of cross-country skis and some duct tape. First, measure 36" from the tip of the skis and saw off the ends. These 2 sections will be the limbs to your bow. Stack the butt ends on top of each other with a 12" overlap and tape together firmly with duct tape. The grip can be contoured to be more comfortable but isn't necessary. Your grip-hand thumb serves as the arrow rest. Finally, carve or abrade notches on each side of the tips 3" down and string with paracord. This bow is best strung recurve-style with the curved tips of the skis facing forward toward your target.

NICKEL FOR YOUR DINNER

You've heard the phrase "A penny for your thoughts?" How about "a nickel for your dinner"? Check out this very cool hack using a nickel, which could very well help you bag some dinner in a survival scenario. Similar to the Spoon Broadhead hack I talked about earlier in this chapter, a nickel is soft enough to be pounded and filed into a deadly arrow point. Pound the top and bottom out first to create the point and the top lashing portion. The middle can be pounded out left and right to broaden the width of the head. Lastly, use a file to quickly sharpen the edges and abrade lashing points. A pocket full of change can provide enough broadheads for an arsenal of arrows. This hack is from my friends Hank Gevedon and Dave Mead of Reptile Toolworks and online at Kentucky River Trading Company (*www.kyrivertradingco.com*).

  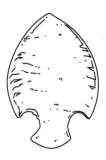

8" PIPE BOW

You can fashion an incredibly powerful bow from a short section of PVC pipe, surgical tubing, and a small square of leather. First, cut 2 10" sections of surgical tubing (or exercise bands). Lash one end of each tube through a hole in the left and right side of the leather patch. This will make a slingshot band set. Finally, wrap-lash or tape the other ends of the tubing along the lower sides of the pipe as shown in the picture. You can load an arrow or dart, draw (as shown), and fire it with incredible force. This makes a suitable low-profile hunting or self-defense bow for a survival scenario. You can also shorten the tubing on a bow of this style to launch much shorter dart arrows for smaller game and birds.

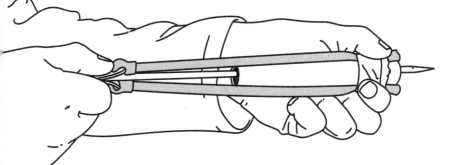

TWEEZERS GIG

Almost every woman I know has a pair of tweezers in her purse. Not only are they good for removing splinters, but you can also use them to catch a frog! Bullfrogs are an amazing survival food source in spring and summer months, but catching them can be quite a challenge. Traditionally, frogs are hunted with barb-pointed trident gigs. When paired with a flashlight to momentarily blind the frog, this is an extremely effective method. Lash a pair of tweezers to the end of a thin, strong stick to make a very effective two-pronged frog gig. Tweezers are sharp and pointed to begin with so no sharpening is necessary. Because tweezers don't have barbs, you have to stab and hold the frog in place and reach down and grab it with your hand. It will slip off your tweezers gig if you try to pull it up from the pond or riverbank.

SLINGSHOT WHISKER BISCUIT

Any slingshot can quickly be converted into an arrow-shooting sling bow with one very simple addition—a paintbrush. Cut a ½"-wide depression from the bristles of a 2"-wide paintbrush to create a perfect whisker biscuit cradle for a full-sized hunting arrow. The cut notch in the paintbrush bristles will create an arrow rest, and the arrow fletching will slide through the bristles without hesitation. Pinch the arrow nock in the slingshot pouch, pull back, aim, and fire. Although the brush can easily be taped in place, a Velcro strap makes putting it on and taking it back off a breeze in the field. A hunter can switch from steel shot to hunting arrows in a matter of seconds without having to carry a roll of duct tape. This hack is from my friends Hank Gevedon and Dave Mead of Reptile Toolworks and online at Kentucky River Trading Company (*www.kyrivertradingco.com*).

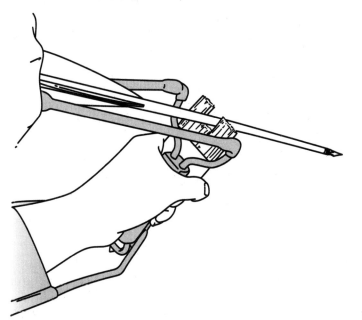

DAVID'S SLING FROM YOUR SHOES

Your 2 shoestrings and 1 of your shoe tongues can make a sling powerful enough to bring down a giant (or small game for dinner). Cut your shoe tongue in an eye shape; about 4" long, tapered on each end and 2" wide in the middle. Punch a hole in the left and right side. Tie a 36" piece of shoelace to each side. Tie a loop using a bowline knot (*www.willowhavenoutdoor.com/bowline-knot*) on one end of one of the laces and an overhand knot (first knot when you tie your shoes) on the end of the other. Place the loop around the ring finger on your throwing hand and pinch the overhand knot between your thumb and index finger. Load the pouch with a smooth rock, sling above your head, and release the knot when you want to launch the projectile. This hunting tool can be very effective, but you'll need a ton of practice to become accurate with it.

IMPROVISED ARROW FLETCHING

Almost any lightweight straight wooden shaft can be fashioned into an arrow for hunting. The ones shown have been split and shaped out of a board from a shipping pallet. After smoothing it and nocking it at the end with a saw, it's time to add the fletching. The fletching is the feathers on the arrow that stabilize it and help it to fly straight. A fletching is critical to the accuracy of any improvised hunting arrow. I know of three outstanding fletching hacks. Cardboard, shown first, can be trimmed and glued into place as shown. Duct tape can also be applied as shown to make a great arrow fletching. Finally, almost any thin rope or ribbon can be tied on as shown to help stabilize an arrow. This hack is from my friends Hank Gevedon and Dave Mead of Reptile Toolworks and online at Kentucky River Trading Company (*www.kyrivertradingco.com*).

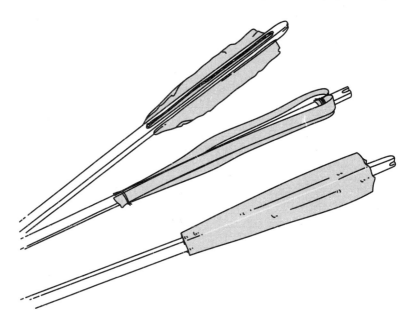

KEY TO EATING WILD GAME

You may not have nice store-bought, razor-sharp broad-head arrow tips in a survival scenario, but chances are you'll have your house keys in your pocket. Believe it or not, the key to your house can also be your key to dinner. All that's required is a regular run-of-the-mill metal file. The key can be shortened by ½" to reduce bulk and weight and the tip sharpened. Then, file the left and right sides to a razor edge. Lashing points can be filed around the edge of the base and then you can lash the key into the end of a wooden shaft to make a very effective metal-tipped hunting arrow. This hack is from my friends Hank Gevedon and Dave Mead of Reptile Toolworks and online at Kentucky River Trading Company (*www.kyrivertradingco.com*).

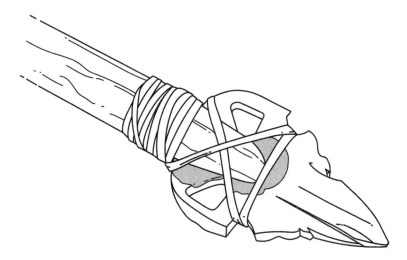

CARPET QUIVER

After you've made arrows using some of the hacks previously mentioned, you'll now need a quiver to put them in. A water bottle, a scrap piece of carpet, and a roll of duct tape can make a very durable and functional quiver. Roll a water bottle (at the bottom) and a roll of duct tape (at the top) in a scrap piece of carpet or even an old welcome mat and wrap it with cord to hold everything together and to provide a shoulder sling. The roll of duct tape makes for a solid opening, and the water bottle (with the top cut off) makes a good puncture-proof bottom. This quiver is lightweight, easy to make, and will safely hold up to 10 arrows with no problem. This hack is from my friends Hank Gevedon and Dave Mead of Reptile Toolworks and online at Kentucky River Trading Company (*www.kyrivertrading co.com*).

BALLOON BOTTLE SLING

The most basic of dart or rock slings can be manufactured from a balloon and the neck of a trash plastic bottle. First, cut the neck off the bottle a few inches below the mouth. It should resemble a small funnel. Remove the cap and stretch the mouth of the balloon over the threaded bottle opening and wrap cordage around the balloon to hold it tightly over the grooved threads where the cap would twist. Place a dart or ball bearing through the large end of the bottle and pinch it between your index finger and thumb inside of the balloon. Hold the neck of the bottle with one hand and retract the projectile back as far as you can pull. When released, the elasticity of the balloon will fire the dart or ball bearing with enough force to kill small birds or distract a stalking man or beast.

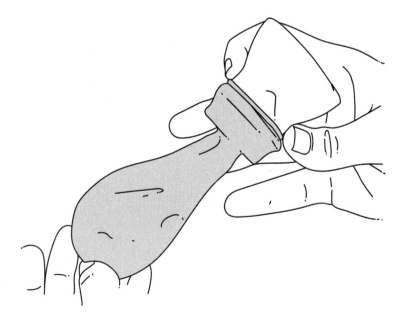

A BETTER MOUSETRAP

Although mice aren't a choice wild-game meat, they can make good bait (live or dead) for a variety of larger game. You can make a very effective mousetrap from a 5-gallon bucket, a straight rod (either metal or wood), a water bottle or wheel, and some peanut butter (or other bait). Thread the wheel or water bottle over the straight rod so that it freely rotates with just a touch. Drill a hole on each side of the bucket with your knife so that the rod and spinning wheel/bottle is suspended in the center. Smear some peanut butter on the wheel/bottle and place a stick or board ramp to the edge of the bucket. When a mouse climbs up the ramp and jumps to eat the peanut butter the wheel/bottle will spin and dump the mouse into the bucket, where he will remain until you come back to retrieve him.

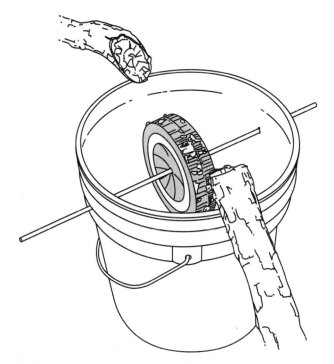

25-CENT MOUSETRAP

I've used mice to catch everything from fish and opossums to snakes and raccoons. Nearly everything in the forest will feed on mice when given the opportunity. One of the simplest mousetraps ever hacked involves just a quarter, a glass, and some bait such as peanut butter. Turn a wide-mouth drinking glass upside down with its front lip propped on the top of a quarter standing on its side. It may be tricky to balance at first, but this "hair trigger" is neces-sary. With bait placed under the glass, a mouse must scurry inside and past the quarter to take it. The slightest bump of either the quarter or the glass and the trap col-lapses, enclosing the mouse inside a glass cage. Peanut butter smeared on the inside of the glass will ensure a quick capture. Slide a stiff piece of paper or cardboard under the glass and mouse, and you can transport him with ease.

DEADFALL TRIGGER

A No. 2 lead pencil makes one of my all-time favorite dead-fall trap triggers. I call it the break-notch trigger. Start by sawing a notch in the middle of the pencil that goes exactly halfway through it. Now, turn the pencil over and saw another notch halfway through; this second notch should be about 1" above or below the first notch on the other side. Now, with your thumb on one notch, snap the pencil into 2 pieces. It will almost always snap to create a perfectly mated trigger that makes a very sensitive deadfall trigger. The Toilet Lid Live Bird Capture hack in this chapter describes a great live capture trap using this trigger.

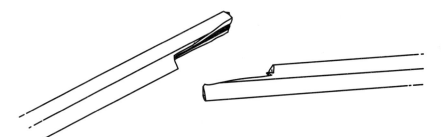

TOILET LID LIVE BIRD CAPTURE

Yes, a toilet lid can catch you dinner! Using bricks or wooden blocks, build an oval frame the same size as the toilet that is anywhere from 2" to 4" tall. When you place the toilet lid on top there should be no major gaps or escape routes. The bricks/blocks will provide a support for the lid. Using the Deadfall Trigger hack in this chapter with the No. 2 pencil, prop up the lid and tie 2 lines of dental floss (or thread) to the bottom half of the trigger stick and then to 2 separate pegs in the ground toward the back of the interior space. Finally, sprinkle seeds or bread inside the trap. When a bird goes into the trap for the bait it will trip the lines, which will collapse the trigger stick and cause the lid to drop, capturing the bird(s) inside.

BUILD A BIRD BOTTLE NOOSE-APULT

Here's a cool hack based on an old bird snare. This cool little trap uses the bottom of a plastic bottle (in the original plan for the trap, it was half a coconut shell) and 2 flexible twigs to launch a noose around a bird's neck. It's a very inventive design that is triggered by a bird's natural pecking behavior.

Start by cutting off the bottom 2" of a normal plastic water bottle (anything up to about 4" in diameter will work). Bury this so that it's flush with the ground. Next bend 2 flexible twigs in an X pattern so they make a crossed arch over the opening of the bottle. (See illustration for details.) Finally, lay an open noose over the flexed twigs around the rim of the bottle and place bait (typically seeds) in the bottom of the bottle. When a bird pecks for the seeds it disturbs the bent twigs, which cast the noose upward around the bird's neck. The bird will jump when the twigs release, and this action will cinch the noose tight.

THE 2-LITER SPOON

Did you know a 2-liter pop bottle can yield 5 spoons? If you look closely you will see several spoon bowl shapes along the bottom. Cut out one of those extrusions along with an extended piece as a handle to extract a nearly perfect spoon for wild soups and stews or scavenged urban canned goods. The leftover top of the 2-liter bottle makes an excellent bowl with the cap on or a funnel with the cap removed. Did you know the mouth of a 2-liter bottle fits perfectly into the fuel tank of a car or truck for an emergency refueling funnel?

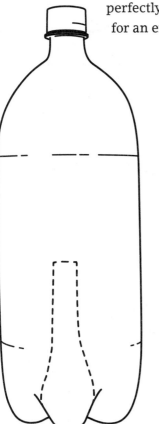

LOOP STICK POT HANGER

A long, flexible tree branch can be quickly converted into a pot-hanging tool. Start by cutting off a branch less than ½" in diameter just below a Y junction. Trim the shorter of the two Y branches to only 2" long. Bend the other, longer Y branch into a loop and lash it back on itself, using a whip knot. This loop can be slid over a traditional spit stick, and a pot can be hung from the 2" Y hook that dangles below.

Multiple hangers can be made at different heights for a variety of cooking temperatures or pots. *Note*: Basswood, mulberry, maple, beech, and willow all make excellent loop stick pot hangers. In spring, you can use the bark of the basswood, mulberry, or willow as the lashing cordage.

SHOVEL IT IN

Have you ever heard the phrase "shoveling it in" referring to someone who is eating ravenously? This hack gives a new meaning to that expression. In the absence of a good skillet or griddle to use for survival cooking, several farm tools will work quite nicely as substitutes. Many believe that the term "hoecake" got the name because workers baked little corn cakes on the blades of their hoes while on break from tending the fields. A metal shovel makes a fantastic cooking griddle for meats, vegetables, and breads. The long handle is also very convenient for maneuvering a meal in and around the fire. I've cooked many a meal in the bush on my foldable pack shovel. A rake and pitchfork also make excellent skewers for roasting meats.

A NEW "RIND" OF COOKING

If you're lucky enough to find a pumpkin, squash, or edible gourd in a survival scenario, don't slice it up to eat too fast. You can simmer a fine woodsman stew inside the hollowed cavity. Meats, root vegetables, greens, and of course the flesh inside the container itself can all be boiled and stewed inside the caldron rind. After you've eaten this fine stew and inner flesh, use the rind several more times to boil and purify water or to make additional wild stews. *Note*: Pumpkin seeds can be roasted on a hot rock and make a nutritious trail snack for a survivor on the move.

NATURAL ALTERNATIVE TO ALUMINUM FOIL

One of my favorite childhood meals was what my mom called a Hobo Dinner. It was hamburger, potatoes, carrots, and onions wrapped in aluminum foil and baked in the coals of a fire. Tin foil is a perfect medium for baking meats and root vegetables in a hot coal bed. This type of cooking also lends itself very well to a survival scenario because you can do other chores while the food cooks. A natural hack to replace aluminum foil is leaves. They have to be green and nonpoisonous. My favorites are basswood, burdock, cattail, and maple. Wrap your food in 3–4 layers of leaves and tie like a birthday package with strips of green willow, mulberry, or basswood bark. Your food will bake inside exactly like in aluminum foil.

FORK HANDLE HACK

From tuna cans to Christmas cookie tins, improvised cooking pans and pots can be made from all different shapes and sizes of metals tins. However, none of them come with convenient handles. You can make a quick and sturdy handle from a regular kitchen fork. Poke 4 holes in the top rim of the tin with your knife, insert the fork tines into those holes, and bend them in an alternating pattern. This provides a safe, sturdy handle for adjusting and lifting the pot in and out of the cooking area. Placing the tin over a stump or log end allows you to poke the holes through the tin and into the wood with ease.

BOTTLE CAP SCALER

When processing several fish for a large group of survivors, it's always better to split the task up to save time and energy. If there's only one knife available for gutting and cleaning, a team can save time by scaling the fish first using an improvised bottle cap scaler. The sharp, ribbed texture of the bottom of a bottle cap is the perfect tool for the job. Nail the cap (bottom out) to a stick or piece of wood and work it against the scales to quickly remove them. The first person in the processing line can scale, and the second can gut and clean. This makes for a very quick and efficient fish-cleaning arrangement.

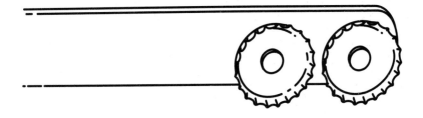

POT HANGERS

Here's a hack that requires almost no product modifications. If you're an inexperienced camper and need to learn knife skills, it can be a little tricky to hang a pot of stew or water over the fire to boil without some carefully notched sticks. Sometimes, creativity can trump skill in survival, and this is a prime example. Hang a run-of-the-mill wire hanger upside down over a tripod with the hook wrapped around the pot bail. It may not be the bushcraftiest pot hanger in the world, but it sure is one of the fastest hacks I've ever used. In survival, it doesn't matter how it looks; it only matters how it works.

DASHBOARD DEHYDRATOR

On sunny days, the dashboard beneath the big front windshield of a car can get seriously hot. In fact, it's plenty hot enough to dehydrate meat and vegetables. Dehydrating anything requires some ventilation, so you'll have to crack the windows a little bit. If flies are an issue, be sure to cover the cracked windows with some mesh or screen.

Cut meat, fruits, and vegetables in thin ¼" strips and then place on the dash on raised drying racks that have at least 2" of clearance for airflow. Any type of mesh or grid trays will work when propped up on small blocks. On an average sunny day meat can be ready to eat in 6–8 hours. Fruits and vegetables can dehydrate even sooner. The addition of a solar-powered fan on the dash can expedite the process. Even when the outside temperature is in the sixties, vehicle interior temperatures can exceed 115°F.

CLAY POT COOLER

Although there is no hack substitute for a good refrigerator, I can show you how to make a very effective evaporative cooler that can extend the shelf life of fruits, vegetables, and other perishable foods. It all starts with 2 porous flower pots, one slightly larger than the other. Standard terra cotta pots work great. First, plug the hole at the bottom of the large pot and fill the bottom with enough sand to raise the top rim of the smaller pot level with the top rim of the larger pot. Second, fill the space in between the pots with sand, then pour in water so that the sand is completely saturated. The evaporation of the water through the outer pot draws heat from the inside of the smaller container, cooling whatever is inside. It helps to place the cooler in a breeze to increase convection. A damp towel over the top of the cooler serves as the perfect lid.

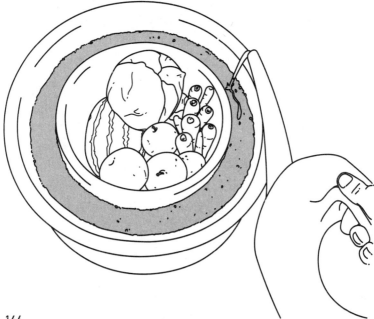

MINI SOLAR DEHYDRATOR

Dehydrating meat to make jerky is a preservation method that every outdoorsman or outdoorswoman should be familiar with. Meat can last for months when the moisture has been removed and the meat has been made into jerky. You can fashion a very simple mini dehydrator from an empty Pringles snack container. The inside of these cylindrical tubes is coated with a silver reflective foil, which is perfect for making a mini solar dehydrator. First, cut a section about 2" × 8" out of the side of the container. Cover the resulting hole with a section of mesh from an old screen window or door to prevent flies from coming inside. This also allows for good airflow, which is very important when making jerky. Put your meat on a skewer and suspend it from 2 holes punched in the lid and in the bottom of the Pringles tube. One day in full sun should be all you need to make a skewer of jerky. This hack solar dehydrator is capable of reaching the ideal dehydrating temperatures of 130°F–170°F. Your jerky is ready when it cracks when bent in half.

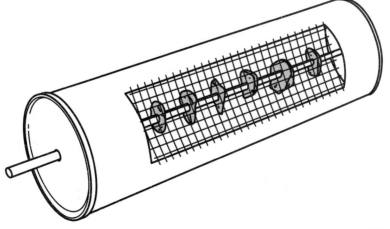

Chapter 5

Staying Healthy

HYGIENE HACKS

SELF-DEFENSE HACKS

Nothing else matters when you don't have your health. This is certainly true in a survival scenario. Even the simplest injury to a hand or eye can be devastating when you're fighting to provide yourself with shelter, water, fire, and food. From sunburn to broken bones, much in this chapter is dedicated to hacking yourself back together in the event of an incident requiring first aid.

As many a doctor will say, "The best cure is prevention." This is certainly true in a survival scenario when access to medical facilities and supplies may be limited, or nonexistent altogether.

Some scenarios are more dangerous than others. Certainly, large-scale natural disaster and civil unrest top the list. It's not hard to imagine an event that might call for some degree of self-defense. This chapter concludes with hacks using everyday objects that can be used to protect you from nature, beasts, and your fellow humans.

DUCT TAPE SNOW GOGGLES

Snow blindness (photokeratitis) is a very real phenomenon. Imagine sunburn-like symptoms except they occur on your cornea. It's not only painful but it can literally blind you until it heals several days later. Hacking an Inuit-inspired pair of snow goggles is the best solution. First, tear off 2 6" strips of duct tape and stick them together, sticky side in. Then cut 2 slits where the eyes will be. Lastly, attach a head strap by poking holes on each end of the duct tape goggles. The slit reduces the eyes' exposure to sunlight and thus helps to prevent a burn on the eyeballs. Dark fabric, leather, and bark can also be used instead of duct tape.

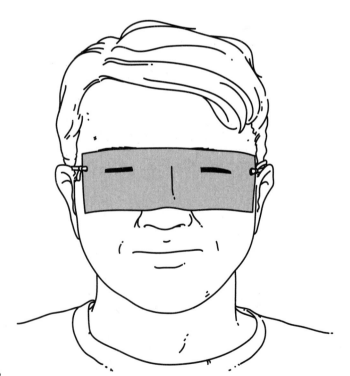

PLASTIC BOTTLE SPLINT

If you know much about construction, then you may know that curves are very strong. Even thin materials become very strong and rigid when shaped into a C trough shape. For this reason, many of the world's bestselling splints for broken and fractured limbs are in the form of a C. Almost all round plastic bottles can quickly be converted into this shape. Trim off the top and bottom of the bottle, then smash and force the upper half into the lower half's curve. This will make for a very sturdy trough-style splint. If you want to make the splint even more rigid or longer, sandwich several bottles together. Place this splint over the extremity and lash it into place to reduce movement and protect the injury during travel.

HEEL DRIVING—A WALKING HACK

Although this tip doesn't use an everyday object, it's what I will call a *walking hack*. Over the years I've seen too many people fall while descending a steep grade, some injuring themselves. There is an effective method of walking down very steep hills that many do not know. I learned this as a small child from a man in the logging industry who spent most of his life wrangling trees on Kentucky's steep ridges.

Most people walk sideways down a steep grade, which feels safer but is actually very dangerous. It's almost always more difficult to recover from a sideways fall, and knee, hip, and ankle joints prefer not to bend sideways. The proper way is to drive the heel in the ground while stepping down the hill face forward. The heel creates a small stairstep and prevents the foot from slipping on forest duff at a steep angle. This works very well with and without snow.

2-JACKET STRETCHER

Hauling an unconscious or injured survivor out of the woods is no easy task. In certain cases (especially with a broken neck or back) using a stretcher is the safest and more effective method. In the absence of a strong tarp that can be used for the body of the stretcher, 2 jackets will work just fine. First build a rectangular framework using 4 saplings and tying a square lashing at the corners. Next, slide the jackets over the length of the framework, end to end, with the zippers or buttons closed. Once the jackets are in place, tie the arms together on the back side to pull the front of the jackets taut across the frame. This arrangement should be strong enough to carry even an adult male to safety.

HACK YOUR TEMPERATURE WITH A WET BANDANA

The body is a radiator, and blood is the coolant. During times of extreme heat or overexertion, a wise woodsman can trick the body into cooling down by wetting and exposing the areas where blood runs close to the skin, called pulse points. A cool, wet bandana applied to the temples (temporal), neck (carotid), front side of the elbow (brachial), wrists (radial), inner thigh (femoral), back of the knee (popliteal), and inner ankle (posterior tibial) can cool the blood running close to the surface in those areas and therefore help to cool the entire body. In cool climates, insulating the pulse points can have a warming effect. Your fingers are often cold not because of poor circulation but because your wrist is exposed and the blood is not providing necessary warmth to the fingers.

BRA CUP DEBRIS MASK

Toxic ash and debris can be a serious problem during natural or manmade disasters. Breathing in ash, pulverized concrete, and debris particles can slow you down as well as result in severe long-term conditions such as asthma and lung cancer. Most women carry 2 hack debris masks on their person at all times—a bra! The padded cups of most bras fit perfectly over the mouth and nose and can act as a crude debris filter in an emergency. The combination of foam, padding, and 2 layers of fabric is much better than most store-bought masks. You can rework bra straps and ties to hold the mask securely on your face for hands-free travel.

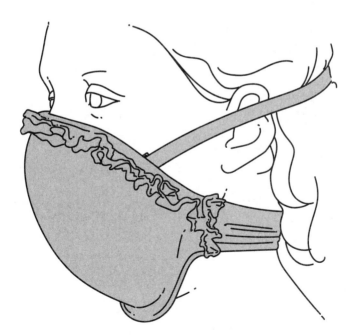

CHARCOAL TUMMY AID

Activated charcoal is an effective treatment in the emergency room for poison victims. Activated charcoal tablets can be purchased at almost any pharmacy and are known to absorb toxins, poisons, chemicals, and the like in your system. Charcoal has the unique ability to "attach" to these elements and carry them through your system. The chemical makeup of charcoal is such that it has an incredible amount of attachment points. This is why charcoal is an ingredient in almost every water filter on the market. If you're in a survival scenario and have a severe stomachache, chances are you won't have fancy activated charcoal tablets. However, a next best solution is to crush hardwood charcoal (the black stuff, not white ash) from the fire and make a drink. Mix about 2 teaspoons of crushed charcoal with 1 cup of water for a natural stomach pain reliever.

COTTER PIN TWEEZERS

This is another hack from the days of my grandfather. Cotter pins are split pins found on all types of machinery, designed to be used as fasteners. The end of a cotter pin can be filed to a razor-sharp point either with a metal file or an abrasive rock. Because a cotter pin is split into 2 halves, it can be used as a very effective pair of tweezers. By spreading the tines and inserting a dowel, the sharp working ends can be bent inward and used exactly like a traditional pair of tweezers. Cotter pins can be found in every hardware store as well as on farm equipment and lawnmowers. They are often used to hold the tires in place on garden wagons and wheelbarrows.

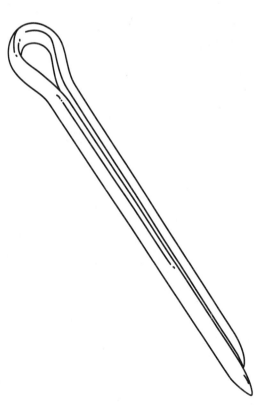

ORBIT GOGGLES

Several years ago, Orbit chewing gum introduced a cup-style package that fits perfectly in most vehicle cup holders. As I was about to throw one away the other day I noticed how the clear lid resembled a pair of welding goggles. After sourcing another lid and experimenting with some cord I was able to fashion a very suitable pair of protective goggles. The little flap door for popping out a piece of gum serves double duty as a vent to prevent fogging in cold weather. I'll admit that they resemble the wardrobe from *Mad Max*, but I have no doubt they'll protect the eyes from flying debris, branch slaps, dust, and sand. After an injury to my eye several years ago while camping I will never underestimate the importance of eye protection again.

MAKESHIFT BUTTERFLY BANDAGE

Here's a quick and easy first-aid hack you may never have seen. I learned this one from an Army field medic while taking a wilderness first-aid class a few years back and thought it was great. As you know, bandages are a luxury in a survival scenario and you want to make the best possible use of them when necessary. Often, especially on the hands, fingers, and knuckles, traditional bandages just don't work that well. To make them more flexible and adaptable, cut a center slice through each of the adhesive strips long-ways from the ends up to the bandage portion. Now, with 4 adhesive strips instead of 2, you can apply the bandage effectively to stubborn body parts.

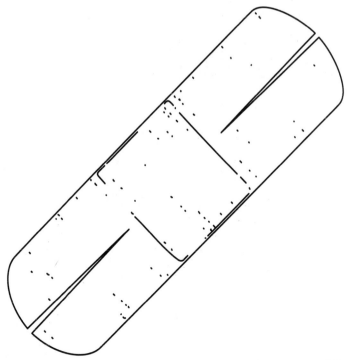

A BETTER-THAN-NOTHING SOUP CAN GAS MASK

Many do-it-yourself gas masks have 2 main ingredients that help to filter out harmful chemicals/gases: activated charcoal and soda lime. The activated charcoal helps to trap particles as they pass through the breathing element, and the soda lime helps to neutralize acid gases. Equip yourself with a better-than-nothing gas mask in a pinch by packing an empty soup can with half crushed charcoal from a fire and half baking soda (sodium bicarbonate). Neither will perform as well as activated charcoal and soda lime, but both are better than nothing. Take one end completely off of the soup can. Cut a hole and insert a plastic pipe 1" into the other end. Duct-tape it in place so there are no leaks. Pack some paper towels or a rag firmly in the soup can against the pipe opening. Loosely pack the rest of the can with half crushed charcoal and half baking soda and tape another rag on the top to hold it all in place. Breathe in through the pipe and exhale through your nose.

SURVIVAL EYEBLACK

As mentioned in the Duct Tape Snow Goggles hack in this chapter, taking steps to prevent eye burn from the sun or snow can be critical to survival. A very effective way to hack your own survival eyeblack in the field is to mix some lip balm with crushed charcoal. Although the wax-based balm will work, petroleum jelly–based products work even better. Smear the greasy "paint" beneath your eyes to prevent sun glare and also improve visibility in both desert and Arctic conditions.

2-LITER SAFETY GOGGLES

I consider safety goggles a necessity in any disaster survival scenario. The ability to quickly make a pair from trash is a great skill to have. A trash 2-liter bottle is the perfect hack for this. The curved contour of the bottle makes a pair of light-duty safety goggles that naturally curl around your eyes and face without the use of a tie or elastic strap. Using a knife or scissors, cut a 2" section from the center of a 2-liter bottle. Next, make a top-to-bottom slice through one side so that you can open up the circle. Carve a groove for the bridge of your nose, and line the edges with tape for a comfortable fit. The ends can be tapered like a pair of sunglasses if you find that more comfortable. A head strap is optional but recommended.

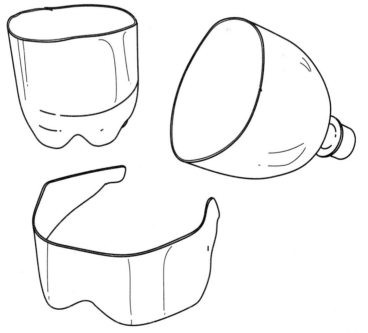

THE BEST NATURAL MOSQUITO REPELLENT

Mosquitoes are arguably worse in the North Woods. Many woodsmen from Michigan or Alaska will tell you that the mosquito is their state bird. Ironically, one of the best natural mosquito repellents is only found in the North Woods—birch oil. The trick is extracting birch oil from the white, papery bark of the birch tree. To do it, you'll need 2 cans. One should be approximately the size of a 1-gallon paint can with a lid and the other about the size of a small soup can. Fill the large paint can with birch bark, put on the metal lid, and then punch a hole in the center bottom. Bury the small can in the ground so that the open top is flush with the ground and place the larger bark-filled can directly on top of it so that the hole is over the smaller can. Finally, build a fire around the large can and let it burn for about 30 minutes. The heat will extract the oil from the bark, which will drip into the smaller can below. Smear this oil on your skin to repel mosquitoes.

A NOT-SO-STRAWEFUL TICK PULLER

Ticks are nasty critters and the bane of many a woodsman. The best way to rid yourself of ticks is to pinch the head with tweezers and pull upward with steady, even pressure. In the absence of suitable tweezers, make a tick puller from a plastic drinking straw. Using a knife or scissors, cut an eye-shaped hole toward the end of the straw large enough to fit over the tick's body. The outside tip of the eye cut (the side closest to the edge of the straw) should come to a very fine point. Slide the eye over the tick and pull from the side, wedging the tick's head and neck in the corner of this fine-cut point. Steadily pull until the tick detaches, and then wash the affected area with soap and water.

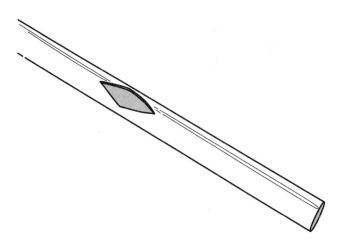

HORSEFLY SHOTGUN

Black flies and horseflies can be a force to be reckoned with during hot summer months. When I was a boy, I learned a simple and fun trick to quickly and easily kill them. It happened by accident at the beach. Whenever we went to the beach I would bring my slingshot so that I could launch dog food kibbles into the water for fish to eat. While I was playing in the sand, the black flies and horseflies were driving me crazy. I noticed a big horsefly that landed on my sand castle, and having run out of dog food kibble ammunition, I filled my slingshot pouch with a pinch of beach sand and blasted him from nearly 5' away. The sand dispersed in a shotgun effect when launched from the slingshot, and I quickly discovered that I could kill any black fly or horsefly within a 10' radius—even flying!

BBQ SPIT BATH

This hack comes from one of my favorite movies of all time—*The Book of Eli*. Prepackaged wet naps that you'll often find at BBQ restaurants make perfect mini spit bath towelettes. I keep a couple in most of my survival kits for just that purpose. They are typically free, weigh almost nothing, and do not expire as far as I've noticed. Two wet naps make for a pretty decent spit bath. There is a bit of a science to mini towelette spit bathing. Use the first one for your face, neck, armpits, and feet, in that order. Use the second for your unmentionables, front to back. If you wish to reuse, boil to sterilize in a small cup or can of water and repeat.

ULTRALIGHT CLOTHESPINS

All clothing becomes less efficient when the fibers are clogged with dirt, grime, and oils. They lose breathability and insulating properties, which are both important features to warm- and cold-weather survival. Washing clothing may become a necessity in order to maintain good field hygiene. Drying your wet clothes on a line in the sun or by the fire can be a little tricky if the wind picks up. I recently discovered the coolest little lightweight clothespins while I was making a peanut butter and jelly sandwich of all things. Plastic bread bag clips are the perfect shape for clipping a garment onto a paracord drying line. The rigid hooks hold the garment tightly and securely even during wind gusts. I've added a few to my bug out bag just in case! *Note:* A bread bag clip can also prevent the toe thong from pulling through on your camp sandals. Just slide it between the bottom of the shoe and the button on the end of the toe thong.

RIOT MASK

Whether you find yourself in the middle of a riot, terrorist attack, or severe natural disaster, the ability to make a quick and effective improvised protective face mask is an invaluable skill. A really impressive mask can be made from almost any large clear plastic water bottle or gallon jug, some duct tape, string, and a T-shirt.

Cut off the bottom of the container and then the back side as shown in the illustration. Foam weather stripping works great to seal the edges around your face, but duct tape is a good next-best solution. Stuff a T-shirt into the neck of the bottle to act as a filter and remove the cap. Finally, pierce 4 holes (2 on each side) in the mask and use string to tie it tightly against your face. This not only helps to protect your eyes and face from flying debris but also helps to prevent the inhalation of smoke and toxic ash.

TWISTED PARACORD PERIMETER ALARM

Paracord can be wound and twisted to make very effective trigger systems for both traps and perimeter alarms. This hack will demonstrate how it can be attached to a tripwire to alarm you when someone is approaching your camp. Start by tying 2 pieces of paracord between 2 small trees. The ideal distance between trees is less than 2'. Insert a stick between the 2 pieces of paracord and twist until the line develops enough pressure to spin when you let it go. Place your tripwire across the trail and attach the end of the line to the lower portion of this trigger stick with a loop while it is wound very tightly. The taut tripwire and loop will hold the trigger stick in place. Finally, hang a cluster of empty cans so they dangle in the path of the spinning trigger stick. When the line is disturbed the loop will be pulled from the bottom and release the spinning trigger stick into the cluster of cans, sounding the alarm.

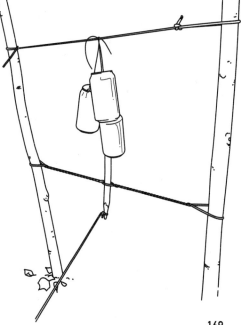

SMOKE ALARM PERIMETER GUARD

Bedding down at night can give even the bravest outdoorsman a vulnerable feeling. Setting a perimeter alarm around camp is one way to outsmart an intruder, either man or beast. You can hack a smoke alarm and clothespin to make a startling perimeter alarm.

Remove the buzzer (including wires), battery, and battery tray (including wires) from a smoke alarm. The buzzer and battery tray should each have a black and red wire. Extend the red wire of both the alarm and battery tray with some additional scrap wire and wrap the other end of one wire around the top pincher of the clothespin and the other wire around the bottom pincher. When the pincher closes the wires should touch. Now, connect the black wires from the alarm to the battery tray. When the battery is attached and the clothespin is closed, the alarm should sound. It should stop when the clothespin is open. To set, place a piece of cardboard or wood scrap in the clothespin and attach to a tripwire. When this sliver of material is pulled out, the wires will connect and the alarm will sound.

55-GALLON BATTLE SHIELD

With luck, you'll never be involved in a situation when you need to navigate through a dangerous city or riot. However, if it happens, you may consider packing a shield made from either the front or back half of an empty plastic 55-gallon drum. Once the drum is sawed in half, you can drill holes to attach rope handles for maneuvering and stabilizing. A 55-gallon drum shield can deflect arrows, rocks, slingshots, debris, and even small-arms fire. It may provide the protection necessary to move through hostile streets. These shields can also be used as urban camouflage to temporarily hide from threats. A lighter but less durable version of this shield can be made from standard 5-gallon buckets.

CARDBOARD BODY ARMOR

Cardboard is a resource available in almost every urban survival environment. Cardboard sandwiched to a thickness of 1"–2" will reduce the effects of violent attacks, flying debris, and even small-arms fire. A template of the neck and chest can quickly be made to protect your vitals and then tied into place with available rope. Wear this under an overcoat for discretion. Other areas to protect include the back, groin, and thighs. Cut or tie smaller, more manageable pieces to these areas as well or wear them under clothing and hold by compression with tight-fitting clothing.

THE SPORT OF SELF-DEFENSE

Almost every piece of sporting equipment that I can think of, from hockey sticks and baseball bats to facemasks and football pads, can be used in self-defense. A trip to your nearest sports store can outfit you for the worst scenarios. I've often called sports equipment "the poor man's riot gear." A fresh coat of earth-tone or black spray paint can convert a hodgepodge of bright sports colors into a camouflaged outfit ready for the wilderness or streets. In my tests I've seen football pads stop arrows, thrown bricks, slingshot projectiles, and small-arms fire. Add a 5-pound weight tied to a length of rope in one hand and a climber's ice axe in the other and no person in his right mind would come charging in your direction.

FROM PLUMB BOB TO ROPE DART

Handymen or women will recognize what a plumb bob is. It is a pointed weight attached to a rope that is used as a vertical reference line. I doubt, however, that many have heard of a rope dart. It is an ancient Chinese weapon that consists of a long rope (approximately 10') with a metal dart attached to the end. A user can throw the dart at an opponent and then draw it back for another attack. When swung around in circles, a rope dart can be hurled with incredible force. A loop tied around the user's wrist keeps the rope in hand at all times. While a hardware store plumb bob makes a ready-made rope dart (when attached to a stronger rope like 550 paracord), you can use almost any dart-like object as a substitute. To become proficient with rope darts takes quite a bit of practice. You can also use them as improvised grappling hooks to climb trees or scale walls. *Note*: A railroad spike with a hole drilled at the head also makes a great rope dart.

Chapter 6

Gear Hacks

CORDAGE HACKS

GEAR STORAGE HACKS

Gear is necessary for survival. Whether they be modern, natural, or improvised from found materials, tools make survival possible. Even primitive man used gear extensively. From flint blades to plant-fiber cordage and clay pots, a variety of improvised accoutrements made life in the wilderness not only easier but possible.

This chapter is all about using random everyday items to improvise tools and gear that may be used in some way to facilitate survival. Gear is a generic term including containers, cordage, knives, saws, and a variety of hand tools. In certain instances, the lack of gear (or the inability to improvise it) can make the difference between life and death.

Some would argue that maintaining the gear you *do* have is just as important as the gear itself. For this reason you will also find a section about gear repair and maintenance. Whether replacing a knife handle or waterproofing boots, these hacks help to ensure your gear performs when and how you need it.

MAKE A GLASS FILE

I use a file all the time for tool maintenance and sharpening. It's one of the tools I can never do without.

A surprisingly effective file for soft metals, wood, and plastic can be made from a glass bottle and some epoxy. Start by crushing the glass bottle with a rock in between several layers of fabric. Try to crush it as finely as possible until it looks like tiny grains of sand. Next, sift out all of the large and irregular pieces through a piece of screen mesh. At this point you should be left with glass "sand" of around the same consistency. Apply a layer of epoxy to a clean, dry stick or small file-shaped board and press it into the glass dust so that it is fully coated. Once the epoxy has dried, your glass file is finished and ready for action.

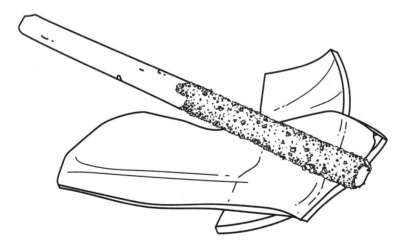

SOUP CAN LID ULU

An ulu is a knife traditionally used by the Inuit and Yupik people of the Arctic. The crescent-shaped blade is specific to that region. It is a blade adapted to the chores of that region, which include skinning game (seals primarily) and cooking and working with caribou hides. The need for carving and chopping is unnecessary due to the scarcity of wood in that part of the world. You can fashion a very solid ulu blade from the tin lid of a standard soup can. Fold ⅓ of the lid over to create a flat, folded edge. Sharpen the exposed rounded edge on a smooth stone. You can use it as is or insert it and lash it into a split stick for a traditional ulu-style grip, as shown in the diagram.

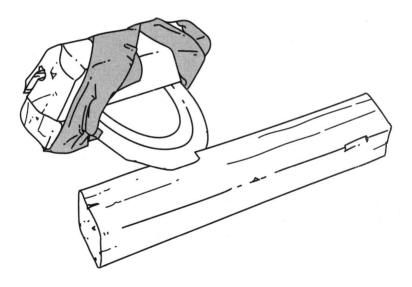

AN *AMAIZE*ING FILE HANDLE

This is a hack I picked up from my grandpa in Kentucky. As a child I used to love rummaging through my grandpa's tobacco barn. It was filled with tons of hand tools that had stories to tell, I'm sure. I'll never forget my grandpa's big wooden crate of files. He used them for sharpening axes, machetes, knives, and farm equipment. Rather than fancy wooden handles affixed to the rat-tail end of the files, grandpa had shoved the files into 5" sections of dried corncob. They made the perfect file handle. The dense inner pith held the file firmly in place and the rough cob made for an awesome grip, even with wet or muddy hands. Dried corncobs make great handles for all kinds of tools including knives, files, and fire pokers.

VIKING CLAMPS

One of the main reasons I carry a multitool as a part of my everyday carry (EDC) is for the pliers. I've learned the hard way that there is no substitute for pliers in the wilderness. This hack, however, is how the Vikings used ingenuity and simple tools to make some very clever clamps that acted as vise grips when building boats. Its simplicity will amaze you.

Sandwich what you need held between 2 boards. Tie a rope around the 2 boards a few inches back from where they are to grip. Then from the opposite end of the gripping end, drive another board or wedge in between the 2 boards. The rope acts as a hinge point, and the gripping end is forced tighter together as the opposite ends are wedged more open. Vikings used this technique to build the hulls of their massive wooden ships, and you can use it too as a makeshift clamping system in a survival scenario.

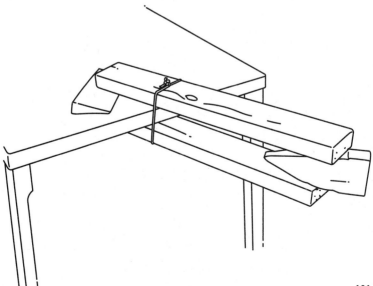

DVD CASE KNIFE SHEATH

There's nothing worse (or more dangerous) than carrying a knife that doesn't have a sheath. As many of you know, Kydex—a thermoplastic that can be heated and molded into almost any shape imaginable—is a very popular sheath material. Black DVD cases can be used as a hack Kydex material. These cases are made from polypropylene and can be heated and molded in a very similar way. Cut the front and back panel off of the case. Heat them over a fire or toaster or in an oven for a few minutes until pliable. When they're nice and soft, sandwich the knife between them and press firmly between 2 folded towels (1 on top and 1 on bottom). Use a book to press the top towel, and do this on a hard surface such as a wood floor. Finally, trim the excess around the sheath with a saw and drill holes for lacing the sheath tightly together with paracord.

COPPER WIRE RIVETS

I learned this hack during a pioneer-living workshop when I was a boy. While fitting a knife blank with a wooden dowel handle, the blacksmith cut short pieces of copper wire and stuck them through one side of the handle, through a hole in the knife handle, and then through the other side of the wood handle. He cut the wire pieces long enough so that they stuck out about ¼" on each side of the handle. He then slowly pounded the copper wire on each side, which caused it to mushroom out and hold the handle tightly in place, just like a rivet. This method of crude riveting can be used in the field to repair a broken knife handle or to replace rivets in another tool that may have worked loose or failed altogether. Metal nails would work as well, but the soft nature of copper makes it a prime candidate for this technique.

ROPE VISE

Sometimes there is no substitute for a good vise when repairing gear or sharpening tools. You can hack a simple foot-powered rope vise. All you need is a picnic table, some rope, and a wooden foot pedal (any old board or stick will do). The picnic table will serve as your workbench.

Start by folding your rope in half, and pull the folded loop up between the boards at the end of the picnic table. Now tie the other 2 ends of the rope together, using a simple granny knot. Make sure that this knot is suspended about 6" off the ground. Complete the vise by placing your pedal stick through the rope loop. Place your knife or tool under the rope loop sticking out the top of your workbench and depress the foot pedal. This will hold your tool firmly in place. The greater the pedal pressure, the tighter the hold.

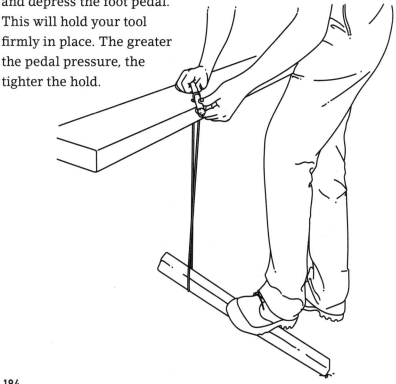

KNIFE-SHARPENING SURFACES

Keeping your blade honed to a razor edge is important. A sharp knife is safer to use and requires less energy. In survival, every calorie counts. You may not know that 2 excellent sharpeners exist almost right under your nose. First is the bottom of a ceramic coffee mug. The bottom ring of most ceramic mugs is almost always unglazed, and unglazed ceramic is a perfect knife-sharpening surface. The underside of toilet tank covers are also unglazed. Then there is the abrasive upper edge of a car window. This edge is sufficient for sharpening most carbon-steel blades. Slide the blade from hilt to tip along the upper edge just as you would use a sharpening rod.

PLASTIC BAG TOOL SHEATH

Scrap plastic grocery bags can be repurposed into durable plastic sheets that can be molded, folded, and sewn into a variety of different pouches, including tool sheaths. Start by cutting the front and back panels from 10–20 plastic bags and lay them flat on top of each other in a pile. It helps to cut out similar rectangular shapes and just throw away the sides, handles, and bottoms. Sandwich this pile of plastic bag sheets between 2 flat rocks. I use large, flat paver stones. Finally, place these stones on the coals of a fire to heat up. As the stones heat, the plastic sheeting welds together into one solid piece of durable plastic that can then be folded and stitched into a very suitable knife sheath. I've also used one of these welded plastic bag chunks as an improvised cutting board with great success. *Note*: You can use a home iron to weld the sheets together. Set to medium heat and place a piece of craft paper on top of and below the stack of sheets.

PLASTIC BOTTLE REPLACEMENT KNIFE HANDLE

This hack involves using plastic high-density polyethylene (HDPE) bottles to make one of the best knife handles I've ever seen. HDPE plastic is marked by a number 2 inside of the recycle sign. Be sure to use bottles/caps labeled with HDPE or with the 2 as its resin identification code because the fumes from other bottles can make you sick.

First, find a metal tube that is about the diameter that you want your knife handle. Cut up the plastic so that the pieces will fit inside of the tube. Fill it full and place near the fire (or in the oven at 350°F) until the plastic melts. Continue to melt pieces until the tube is full. Once the tube is full and the plastic is still in a soft state, press it down using a wooden dowel or plunger to compress out all the air bubbles. Finally, press the knife handle into the tube and let the plastic cool. HDPE shrinks as it cools, allowing you to remove it from the tube when finished. Now, simply carve or file the handle to the shape you want.

IMPROVISED NEEDLE AWL

A sail maker's needle is a good item to keep in survival kits. These are large, thick needles that can be used to make repairs on durable goods such as packs, shoes, canvas pants, and leather items. Sometimes, however, you need an awl to punch through especially thick materials. A good sail needle can be reworked into a great awl by hammering the point ½" into a solid wood handle that you can carve from any hardwood limb. The eye of the needle can now be filed down to a sharp point with a smooth stone or file. The result is a sharp needle with a hole at the tip, which is exactly what an awl is. Thread the eye, push the needle and thread through the materials, and begin your lockstitch pattern.

SKI KNIFE

Ski pole grips are very comfortable, rugged, and durable. They also handle extreme conditions very well. These are all desirable attributes for a knife or tool handle. The process is simple: Slide the handle from the ski pole and fill it with epoxy (it could also be pine resin epoxy made with charcoal—see the Charcoal Epoxy hack in this chapter) and insert the knife or tool. When cured, you've now got a knife or tool with a handle better than most. You can find nice quality rat-tail tang blades (Mora blades are my favorite) online for very affordable prices, and this also makes a fun weekend knife project. You can also use old bicycle handle grips.

CHARCOAL EPOXY

If the need for a strong glue arises and no modern options exist, hack your own using crushed charcoal and pine sap. Start by sourcing pine sap from the pine tree. Often you can find this sap in the form of dried clusters on the exterior of the tree. Look for wounds the tree may have suffered and collect the sap that oozes forth there. Next, melt the pine sap over the heat of a fire in a small metal container or in a depression on a hot rock. While the sap is melting, crush black charcoal from the fire pit (the black chunks, not white ash) into a fine powder. Mix the powdered charcoal into the melted pine sap—1 part charcoal to 3 parts pine sap. As this sticky mixture cools it will harden into a very strong natural epoxy that can be used as a glue substitute. The leftover dried glue in the metal tin can be reheated later to be made pliable once again and used indefinitely.

2-LITER CORDAGE

I saw a video one time about how 2-liter bottles could be recycled to make rope that was ultimately woven into baskets. The process used fancy equipment and electric motors. After seeing it I was determined to figure out a hack way of making cordage from a 2-liter bottle, using only limited tools. After many failed attempts I finally figured out that I could make a few choice cuts in a sapling stump (see diagram) and could then feed a 2-liter bottle through this improvised jig. The result is that I can strip the bottle into cordage that is strong, rot-resistant, and moisture-resistant. To see the full effect of this amazing hack, watch the skills video here: *www.willow havenoutdoor.com/two-liter-bottle-cordage.*

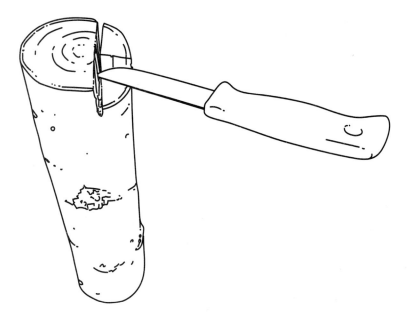

DOG TREAT CORDAGE

Primitive man used rawhide for all kinds of bindings. It was excellent for securing axe and adze heads. Other uses included sewing, bowstrings, shoe bindings, knife sheaths, arrow quivers, shields, drums, furniture, and baskets. Rawhide can also be boiled down to make an excellent glue and is still an ingredient in many modern glues today. Working with rawhide takes practice, but it's not a material that's readily available . . . to a nonhacker. To a creative "hack-minded" survivalist, rawhide practice material is in almost every single grocery store in the form of dog chews and bones. Soak these rawhide chew toys in water until soft and then cut them into cordage or bindings for primitive skills practice. This is a hack that few people consider.

BOTTLE CAP PULLEY

HDPE plastic bottle caps (marked by a number 2 inside of the recycle symbol) can be found all over the place. You can fuse 2 of them to make a very impressive little gear pulley, paired with paracord.

Start by taking 2 equal-sized bottle caps and heat the flat tops until they are gooey enough to be fused together. Placing them upside down on a hot rock for a few minutes should be plenty to do the trick. Press them together and let them cool. The top edge of each cap is slightly rounded, which creates an indented seam around the middle of the fused caps. This will act as your pulley channel. Drill or carve a hole through the middle of the caps to inset an axle, climbing carabiner, or rope loop, and you've got a perfectly functional gear pulley to hoist large game for dressing or send a 5-gallon bucket into a well or over a cliff for water. Using little pulleys like this you can also create some unique cooking cranes.

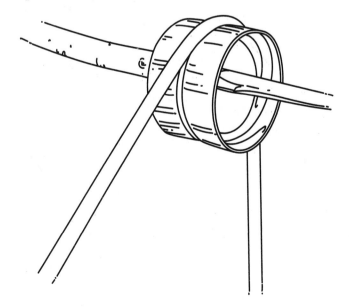

SHOPPING BAG ROPE

Usable rope can be twisted and woven from practically any thin, fibrous material, including plastic shopping bags, ribbons, hair, and plant fibers. In fact, the Incans built grass and natural-fiber bridges that spanned massive rivers and gorges. These bridges supported the weight not only of people but of wheeled carts and livestock. Like most survival skills, the devil is in the details when it comes to improvised cordage. The process of twisting, pinching, and weaving natural (or manmade) fibers into cordage is called the reverse wrap, and this is a hack invented not by myself, but by primitive man many thousands of years ago. I have filmed a video to teach you this skill: *www.willow havenoutdoor.com/reverse-wrap-video.*

USPS WATER-RESISTANT STUFF SACKS

Tyvek is a synthetic waterproof material made from polyethylene fibers traditionally used in the construction industry as a moisture barrier house wrap. Many shipping envelopes, including the ones used for Priority and Express services of the USPS, are also made of Tyvek to protect documents and merchandise from the weather. These envelopes also make great little waterproof stuff sacks. They can be used as is and sealed with the peel-n-stick adhesive strip to protect moisture-sensitive materials, or you can sew a handy drawstring channel around the top edge to make great waterproof gear sack for extended travel. Tyvek is also incredibly light! This is a great way to repurpose used packaging.

SKIVVY ROLL

Packing smart can allow more room in a backpack for important survival gear, so it's always wise to save space whenever and wherever possible. A clean set of underwear, T-shirt, and socks can go a long way in maintaining personal hygiene when normal facilities for washing aren't available. A great hack for packing these 3 items is called the skivvy roll. Packed according to the diagrams, these 3 items are barely larger than just one roll of socks. It really is a genius way to pack, whether going on vacation or arranging your bug out bag.

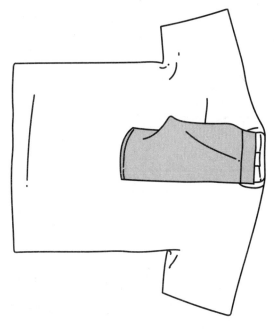

STEP 1

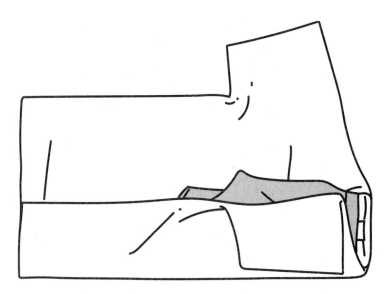

STEP 2

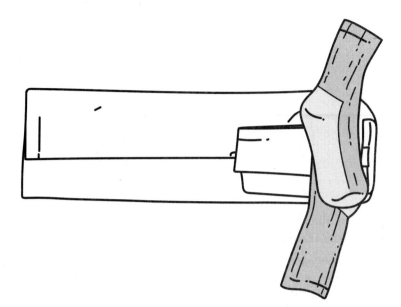

STEP 3

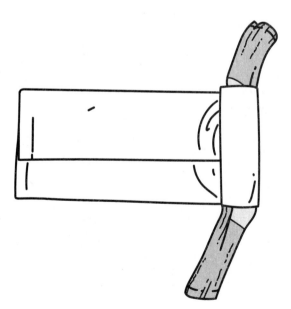

STEP 4

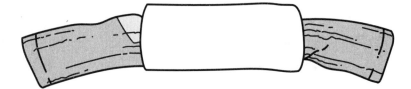

STEP 5

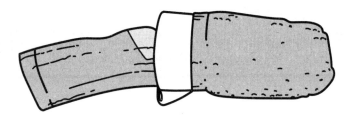

STEP 6

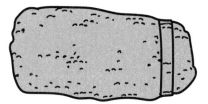

STEP 7

Chapter 7

Forward Movement

Staying put can be a good survival strategy in certain instances, such as when you're lost. However, not having the option to move onward can be downright deadly. This chapter is filled with hacks that provide more options to keep moving forward. Sometimes in survival, movement is life.

Two elements that can stop a survivor dead in his or her tracks are lighting and navigation. In low-light, nighttime, or subterranean environments, the lack of a lighting tool means zero forward movement. Choosing to travel in darkness without a lighting tool can be dangerous and deadly. Without a tool to provide insight into direction, you can walk in circles or, worse yet, in the opposite direction of resources. In survival, every step forward should be with purpose.

The ultimate goal of every survival scenario is to make it out alive. For many, this involves being rescued. This chapter concludes with a small section dedicated to improvised rescue and signaling hacks. Whether during the day, at night, or along a trail, communicating to would-be rescue parties is a critical and valuable survival skill set.

POP CAN LANTERN

The functionality of a modern lantern is very difficult to replicate using makeshift supplies. However, you'd be surprised at how much you can light up a small space with just a candle and a soda can (or any type of aluminum can for that matter). Carefully make 3 cuts in the can using your pocketknife as can be seen in the illustration. Then fold open the "wings" and place a candle inside. The shiny interior surface of the aluminum can reflects and projects the candlelight, creating a lantern effect in a dark room or cave. This can be used to not only navigate a dark building or trail but also to light up a food prep area. If you're traveling, hold the lantern by the bottom where the metal does not get hot or suspend with a handle from the convenient pop tab bail.

HEADLAMP CAMP LANTERN

A headlamp can be quickly hacked into an outstanding camp lantern by placing it around a water-filled bottle using the head strap and with the light shining toward the center. The water diffuses and diverts the light, making a very comfortable camp lantern that can be much more pleasing to the eyes than blinding headlamps around the dinner table. It is also a slightly more discreet way of using a headlamp in the event that you are setting up a stealth camp or trying to remain undetected.

FLASHLIGHT DIFFUSER

Similar to the Headlamp Camp Lantern hack, an empty energy drink bottle with the shrink-wrapping removed can be fitted atop a bright flashlight to make a very functional little camp lantern. A flashlight is designed to project light in one direction in a focused beam. This isn't always the best way to light a survival camp or shelter. Cut the top off of a mini energy drink bottle so that it fits snugly onto the face of a small flashlight. This solid, white plastic body acts like a lampshade to diffuse and spread the light in a much broader area.

LADLE SLUSH LAMP

The term "slush lamp" has dropped from most modern dictionaries—lost in history like so many other important survival skills. It is a crude lamp that typically burns on grease or animal fat. Eskimos used this style of lamp to burn seal blubber. However, the concept and principles can be applied to many different objects and fuels in a survival scenario. This hack uses the slush lamp model and 3 items found in almost any kitchen or grocery store—a ladle, some olive oil, and a strip of cotton fabric. Fill a ladle with olive oil and lay in the cotton strip (a cut piece of T-shirt works great) so that all but ½" is submerged in the oil. The lamp can be lit just like a candle once the ½" of protruding cotton "wick" absorbs the "fuel." A slush lamp of this variety will burn very brightly and for a surprisingly long time.

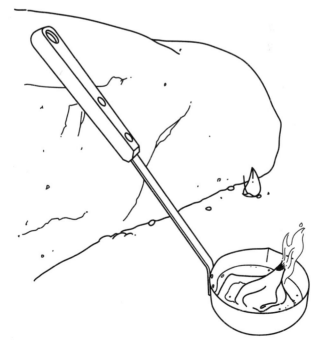

T-SHIRT TORCH

When the sun goes down in the wilderness it's game over without some kind of lighting tool. No flashlight means no work, no movement, and no progress—unless you know how to hack a good torch! It all starts with a fresh-cut green stick 1"–2" in diameter. It must be green because a dead one will catch on fire. Next tear a T-shirt (or any cotton fabric) into 1" strips and wrap those around the end of the stick like a giant Q-Tip. Soak the strips with a low-flashpoint cooking oil such as olive oil. Many cooking oils, including melted butter, margarine, or lard, will work for this. Bacon fat and pine sap are also suitable substitutions. Once the fabric torch head is soaked through, place it in the fire until it catches, and you're good to go. A softball-sized wrap will burn for more than an hour.

CRAYNDLE

What do you get when you light the top of a crayon on fire? A crayndle, of course. Crayons are made up mainly of wax and burn very well. Leave the paper label on because it acts as the crayndle wick. An average crayndle will burn for 30 minutes. To keep them from falling over, melt the pointed writing tip into a small pool on a hard, fireproof surface and place the bottom of the crayon in the melted wax until it cools and hardens. This will prevent the crayndle from tipping or falling over. Need a bigger flame for more light or even cooking? Wrap several crayons together using wire. This will not only produce more light, but it creates a larger flame, which can be used to heat a small space if other types of fuel are limited.

ORANGE YOU GONNA USE THAT PEEL?

I love oranges. Did you know dried orange peels make great fire starters? However, this hack goes beyond using just the peel. An orange peel can actually be used to make a very impressive survival lamp. Peel the orange so that half the peel is intact and that the pithy central column is still attached. At this point the orange should look like a half-hollowed-out orange peel with the pithy core sticking up out of the center. Place the orange on a sturdy, hard, fireproof surface and fill with almost any kind of cooking oil such as olive oil or vegetable oil. The oil will slowly absorb into the pithy center column. After a few minutes, this pithy core can be lit just like a lamp wick and will continue to burn for several hours. *Bonus hack*: One of my favorite camp breakfasts is to bake instant rolls inside half rounds of hollowed orange peels right in the coals of a fire.

CRISCO CANDLE

If your childhood was anything like mine, then you grew up with a big can of Crisco in the pantry. My mom used Crisco for frying and homemade biscuits, but it wasn't until recently that she learned a new use for Crisco: a 30-day candle. Crisco is a solid-state vegetable oil that also happens to burn incredibly well. A Crisco candle is best made with the long strands of a cotton mop head. Cut 1 strand off and cram it down into the can of Crisco using a thin, forked stick. Cut the end that sticks out to about 1" above the top and slather it with a little Crisco before lighting. One can of Crisco can burn up to 30 days. You'll have to replace the wick several times, but it works as an amazing emergency candle. Burn 3 wicks at once for more light and heat. Insert them several inches apart.

WRISTWATCH COMPASS

If you know the time, you can determine direction. Using an analog watch, point the hour hand at the sun. Then, bisect the distance between the hour hand and 12 o'clock. That line, pointing away from the center of the watch, is south. If your watch is digital, just draw a clock with hands on the ground so that the hour hand is pointing toward the sun and do the same thing only on the ground instead of on your wrist.

What if you can't see the sun? Even on cloudy days the sun will still cast a shadow from a stick placed in the ground. Align your hour hand perfectly with that shadow and it will be pointing toward the sun. Continue as just described. Once you know south, the other three directions fall into place.

FINGER CLOCK

This hack isn't so much about finding direction as it is knowing when to stop hiking and start making base camp for the night. Many survivors underestimate how long it can take to set up a proper base camp, and then find themselves rushing around in low-light conditions. A reliable way of estimating the amount of time left until sunset is by using your fingers. Hold your hand up sideways with the bottom of the sun resting on top of your index finger. Now, count the number of fingers going down until they connect with land. Each finger represents approximately fifteen minutes of sunlight available.

AIR GOGGLES

I've placed this hack under the navigation heading because
it's related to navigating underwater. Seeing underwater is
blurry at best without swimming goggles. Air goggles are
simple to make. This is done by creating a tight seal across
your forehead and to the outside of each eye along your
temples with your hands by pressing them tightly against
these areas. When you slowly lower your face into the
water, a pocket of air will collect around your eyes and up
against the wall that your hands create. If there is a small
air leak in your hands, these air pockets can be replen-
ished (or increased in size) by simply exhaling underwater
and adding bubbles to the goggles. Your eyes are now
behind a pocket of air and can see in water just as if you
were wearing goggles. This is a perfect technique for getting a clear view of the bottom of any shallow pool or body
of water.

SHADOWS LEAD THE WAY

You can improvise a fairly accurate compass using just a stick. Even with cloud cover, the sun will cast a shadow. Stab a straight 36" stick into the ground. Mark the end of its shadow with a rock. Wait a couple hours as the sun moves across the sky. Then mark the end of the shadow again with a second rock. Now, draw a line from the first rock to the second rock. This line is the east/west line; the second rock points east. As the sun moves from east to west it casts a shadow from west to east. From this you can then determine north and south.

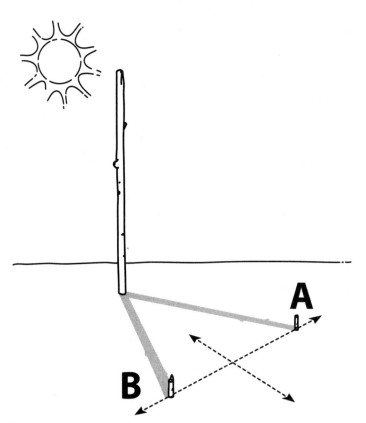

BULLET CASING WHISTLE

Using just an empty bullet casing, a file (or sharp corner of concrete), and a branch, you can make one of the best hack rescue whistles in the world. File a groove ½" from the opening of the bullet casing as shown in the illustration. Be sure the flat 90-degree portion is toward the open end. Next, carve off the top fifth of a branch that is the same diameter as the inside diameter of the bullet casing. Cut this piece so that it is the exact length from the opening to the 90-degree, flat-filed edge and insert it into the end of the casing as shown. This bullet will now produce a piercing whistle to signal for recue.

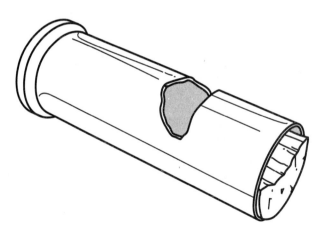

BUSTED CELL PHONE TO THE RESCUE

Let's face it: A cell phone is about the best survival tool you can have—*if it's working!* Everyone knows that technology fails you when you need it most, and cell phones are no exception. Whether waterlogged or broken during a fall, a busted cell phone could still help you signal for rescue. Behind every cell phone screen are several layers of a highly reflective mirror-finish material that can be used to flash the sun's rays in the direction of a rescue party. This works best if you adhere them side by side to bark or a flat rock, using sticky pine sap (wet mud will work temporarily). Increasing the surface area and number of reflective surfaces helps ensure a successful signaling attempt. The best method of accessing these reflective pieces is to crush the phone with a rock from the side, which will split most phones in half with little effort.

GLOW STICK BUZZ SAW

When most people think of a glow stick nowadays what comes to mind are roller rinks, sporting events, or rave dance parties. Although I'm not a big fan of glow sticks for survival lighting, there is a hack way to use one that makes an excellent (and really simple) rescue signal. Tie a 3' length of rope to one end of the glow stick and spin it as fast as you can in a circle facing the direction of your rescue party. At night, this will create a glowing orb, 6' in diameter, that forms an effective visual rescue signal—a big out-of-place moving object. A rescue signal like this one can be seen for miles by a ship or plane. To learn more about this hack, visit *www.willowhavenoutdoor.com/general-survival/ the-buzz-saw-nighttime-survival-signaling-technique.*

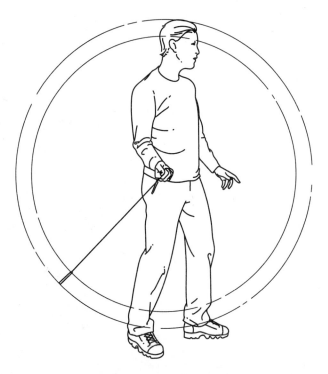

REARVIEW RESCUE

I'll never forget the story of a family lost and stuck in their car in the middle of winter on a snowy logging road. On several occasions, rescue planes flew overhead but the snow-covered car couldn't be seen on the thin road in the dense forest. Survival signal mirrors are a staple recue tool in almost every single survival kit. The reflection of the sun's rays from a signal mirror can be seen for miles by a plane or boat. Even the reflection from a bright moon has been known to save lives. Any mirror or reflective surface will work just fine. A simple hack, if stranded in your vehicle, is to yank the rearview mirror off the window (it's just glued on) and use it to reflect the sun. Vanity mirrors on the visors also work very well.

HANSEL AND GRETEL SURVIVAL

If you're on the move, marking your path of travel has two advantages. First, it allows you to retrace your steps if necessary. Second, it allows a rescue crew to follow your route. A good trail marker should incorporate three elements:

1. It should appear to be manmade. Try not to make a marker that could happen at random in nature.
2. It should have movement if possible. Strips of material hanging from branches that blow in the wind are a prime example.
3. It should indicate your direction of travel.

Two trail marker hacks include a tube of lipstick and an emergency survival blanket. You can shave away the bark of trees to the white cambium layer and draw a lipstick arrow as a marker. An emergency survival blanket can be stripped into hundreds of 1" × 4" strips and hung from branches as glittering signs of travel.

Chapter 8

Everyday Carry (EDC) Kits on a Budget

In general, survival hacking becomes necessary due to a lack of preparation, planning, or both. There is no hacking substitute for proper gear, solid plans, and tested knowledge. One of the best ways to prevent having to hack your way out of a sudden and unexpected survival scenario is to carry some tested survival gear on your person. This is known as an everyday carry (EDC) kit.

At a minimum, you should consider the *core four* categories of survival when building a personal EDC kit:

1. Shelter
2. Water
3. Fire
4. Food

Many survivalists include first aid, tools, and self-defense as core categories as well.

An EDC kit is nondescript, often fitting in pockets, on a key ring, in a purse, on a belt, or in a combination of places. Larger EDC kits can include fanny packs or even backpacks.

An EDC kit can get expensive if you let it. In keeping with the theme of this book, I've decided to dedicate this chapter to EDC on a budget. Look at it as the hack version of an EDC kit. Following, I outline 7 different kits to illustrate that there is no right or wrong EDC build. I hope these spark your own creative ideas, and you can share those with me via e-mail at *creek@creekstewart.com*. Who knows, I may ask if I can feature your idea in a later edition of this book!

EDC ON A BUDGET KIT #1: THE MENTOS CONTAINER POCKET KIT

As mentioned in A Perfectly Minty Lighter Box hack in Chapter 3, an empty Mentos gum container makes an excellent disposable lighter box. I took this a step further and turned one into a full-on survival pocket kit.

CONTAINER:

EMPTY MENTOS GUM CONTAINER

At 3½" × 1½" × 1", this container is rigid, nearly crushproof, and waterproof. It easily fits in a jacket pocket, glove box, or purse. It's lightweight, durable, cheap, and can be opened with one hand. With the label left on, it's also disguised as a container of gum during an unexpected pocket dump.

CONTENTS

1 **3' duct tape.** Wrapped around the outside of the container is 36" inches of duct tape. This can be stripped and used as cordage and also makes very good fire tinder.

2 **Ranger band.** Stretched around the outside of the container is a Ranger band. A Ranger band is simply a crosscut piece of bicycle inner tube. This can be used as weatherproof fire tinder or to hold additional items to the outside of the container.

3 **Mini Bic disposable lighter.** This is one of the most reliable fire-starting tools available. It will work in nearly every survival condition except extreme cold and very high altitudes. Even then it's not completely useless because you can still strike sparks into tinder from the striking wheel.

4 **Folding razor knife.** You can use this little 2" knife to process cordage, clean wild game, gather wild edible plants, and carve trap sets.

5 **Small spool nylon thread.** This was given to me by a friend who works at an automotive manufacturing factory. This is the thread used to sew dashboards together. It's some seriously strong stuff and fits perfectly into the kit. It can be used for fishing line as well as for shelter lashings and guylines.

6 **3 fishing hooks.** Sandwiched between 2 pieces of packing tape, I've included 3 fishing hooks of different sizes. Become comfortable with sourcing live bait, natural bobbers, and rock sinkers. Improvised hooks are very difficult to make and are not effective.

7 **Water purification tablet.** Stuffed in a crack is 1 water purification tablet capable of purifying 1 liter of wild water. This is sealed in a waterproof foil casing by the manufacturer (Aquamira).

8 **6" cotton wick.** I cut 1 6" length of cotton lamp wick in half to make 2 3" sections. These off-the-shelf cotton lamp wicks make excellent fire tinder when shredded. It will ignite with just sparks from a ferro rod or broken lighter. Of course, it can also be used to make a crude slush lamp (see the Ladle Slush Lamp hack in Chapter 7).

9 **Sewing needle.** This large sewing needle can be used in conjunction with the strong nylon thread for gear or clothing repairs.

10 Grade **#0000 steel wool.** This very finely shredded steel wool makes an incredible fire starter. Whether with a spark from a busted lighter or short-circuited with a battery, it burns red hot and can be placed into a tinder bundle and blown into flame.

11 **Hunting arrowhead.** This small- or large-game-hunting arrowhead can be used as an arrow point, a spear point, or even a frog/fish gig. The edges are so sharp that it can also be used as a knife if necessary.

EDC ON A BUDGET KIT #2: THE M&M'S MINIS CONTAINER POCKET STRAW KIT

This kit is unique in that every item inside (except three) is contained within sealed plastic straws. I've mentioned using candy tins in previous hacks (see Makeup Aisle to Fire Tinder and Wallet-Sized Fire Squares, both in Chapter 3), but here I've taken it a step further and used straws to contain every survival item except for the water bag, magnifying lens, and mini ceramic knife.

CONTAINER:
EMPTY M&M'S MINIS CANDY CONTAINER

Like the Mentos container, this one is rigid, nearly crush-proof, and waterproof. It easily fits in a jacket pocket, glove box, or purse. It's lightweight, durable, cheap, and can be opened with one hand. It measures 4" × 1" in diameter.

CONTENTS

1 **2 fire straws.** These are plastic straws filled with petroleum jelly–soaked cotton balls. The straws are then welded at the end by heating the plastic and then squeezing with a pair of pliers. They can be cut open and used as tinder and will ignite with even the spark from a broken lighter.

2 Fishing straw. This sealed straw kit was given to me as a gift and contains spider wire, hooks, a sinker, and even a little bobber. It's the most compact little fishing kit I've ever seen and fits perfectly in this kit.

3 Mini ceramic knife blade. This mini ceramic knife blade is rust- and corrosion-resistant and can be used for a variety of small survival cutting chores.

4 3 match straws. Three sealed straw containers with 1 match each. I have glued a match-striking surface to the underside of the container lid.

5 Water purifier straws. Two straws with 2 1-liter water purification tablets each.

6 1-liter water bag. This water bag can be used in conjunction with the water purification tablets to source and purify fresh drinking water.

7 Fresnel lens. Even though matches are included in this kit, a plastic Fresnel magnifying lens slides perfectly along the inside wall of this plastic container. It takes up hardly any space and makes an excellent fire-starting tool on sunny days.

8 Seasonings straw. One straw filled with a mix of salt and pepper. Every wild meal tastes better with salt and pepper.

9 Bouillon straw. One straw filled with a crushed chicken bouillon cube to make a wild stew, which can also be prepared in the 1-liter water bag. You can even hang the water-filled plastic bag over a fire and heat it (even boil in it if you're careful).

EDC ON A BUDGET KIT #3: THE $3 KIT

This is about the least expensive EDC survival kit you can make. It uses several repurposed pieces in order to save money.

CONTAINER:
1-QUART RESEALABLE FREEZER BAG

One quart equals almost exactly 1 liter (.94). This bag is plenty large to contain a variety of survival necessities. Even when stuffed with the following items it easily fits in a jacket pocket, briefcase, or vehicle glove box.

CONTENTS

1 **Paper matches.** You can still get paper matches for free at fairs, festivals, and many restaurants. Although they aren't my top choice for a fire-starting tool, they work fine as long as you keep them dry.

2 **HotHands Hand Warmers.** Not only can one of these little chemically activated hand warmers help keep you warm in a cold-weather environment, but it can also be used to dry out wet matches in a pinch (see the Salvation for Wet Matches hack in Chapter 3).

3 **Half-used spool of dental floss.** To reduce bulk, a spool of dental floss was removed from the plastic housing. Dental floss has a breaking strength of around 25 pounds and can be used as fishing line, gear repair thread, or even as lashing cordage for camp craft and shelters.

4 **2 alcohol prep pads.** As mentioned in the Wallet-Sized Fire Squares hack in Chapter 3, these little alcohol prep pads make great fire starters. They could also be used to sanitize minor cuts and scrapes.

5 **1 Emergen-C packet.** This drink mix packet is packed with vitamins and minerals—all of which help keep you healthy in a survival scenario. It can also be used to flavor nasty-tasting wild water after it's been filtered or purified.

6 **BBQ wet wipes.** As mentioned in the BBQ Spit Bath hack in Chapter 5, you can take an entire spit bath with 2 wet wipes. I grabbed a couple extra during my last visit to Buffalo Wild Wings.

7 **Emergency survival blanket.** This is the most expensive item in the kit at approximately $1. It is a multipurpose item and can be used for a variety of survival functions. It makes a suitable shelter canopy but serves best as a fire reflector when attached to the inside back wall of a lean-to. Because it reflects 80 percent of radiant heat, you can wrap up in it to conserve and reuse body heat. Following is a list of other uses:

- Ground-to-air rescue signal
- Parabolic lens for fire starting
- Poncho
- Waterproof gear cover
- Emergency fire tinder. Yes, it burns like crazy.
- Cordage. I once reverse-wrapped stripped pieces of emergency blanket to hold the weight of a 200-pound adult male.

8 **Repurposed small loaf baking tin.** Next time you're at your grandma's for Thanksgiving dinner, snag one of the small aluminum foil banana loaf tins before it gets thrown in the trash. They can be folded flat and make a great container for boiling (purifying) water, frying meats, or making stews in the wild. Even brand new you can buy 3 for a couple dollars. Besides a sheet of aluminum foil, these are the most compact metal containers I've ever seen.

9 **Homemade energy bars.** You can make some really cheap homemade energy bars with 4 simple ingredients that work perfectly for EDC kits. Mix the following together and smash into the bottom of a small baking pan: ¾ cup rolled oats, 1 cup small chopped dried fruits, ⅓ cup peanut butter, and ¼ cup honey. Once in the pan, freeze until solid enough to cut into small bar shapes. I package mine in sandwich bags. They only store at room temp for a few days, but I recommend eating them before that anyway. I make mine on Sunday and keep them in my EDC backpack to eat throughout the week. If you don't want to spend the time making these, you can buy CLIF Bars, but they will blow your $3 kit budget.

10 **Hacksaw knife.** A great little knife can be repurposed from an old hacksaw blade. First, break, saw, or cut the blade in half. Then, using a file, sharpen the back edge (opposite the saw side) until sharp. Lastly, wrap a handle with duct tape. A piece of cardboard makes a suitable sheath for storage. You'll be surprised at what this "free" knife can do! Of course, the back is a small wood and metal saw too.

EDC ON A BUDGET KIT #4:
THE KEYCHAIN KIT

This is a kit for the person who truly loves micro kits. It doesn't get much smaller than a survival kit on a keychain. With this kit, every ounce and centimeter counts. Look at this kit as the ultralight backpacker's version of a survival kit.

CONTAINER:

CARABINER + PILL CONTAINER + ACCESSORIES

This kit is designed to go on your key ring and is small enough to be clipped on a belt loop or tucked in a pocket. Because of added bulk, I've found it easier to use a climbing carabiner and clip it right on a belt. This also prevents it from being lost, stolen, or snagged off by a rogue branch. The keychain pill container can be purchased for just a few bucks at any local pharmacy. They are designed to carry medication but are perfect for a variety of small water-sensitive materials, including water purification tablets. They come in a huge variety of colors (both plastic and metal) and are very durable.

CONTENTS

1 **Keychain pill capsule.** I keep 2 items in this waterproof capsule. First, a package of 2 Aquamira water purification tablets capable of purifying up to 1 liter of water each. Second, 2 Baddest Bee Fire Fuses. These are cotton fire starters infused with natural beeswax. They can be torn apart and lit with just the spark from a ferro rod or broken lighter (see next item).

2 **Broken lighter striker.** A great little keychain spark striker can be made from a broken or empty disposable cigarette lighter. A defunct lighter makes a good little striker. With the right tinder you can get a fire 10 times out of 10. The empty lighter on this keychain has been modified so it's not only a striker but also a container for wax-infused cotton fire starters. Follow the photo series to make your own. A Ranger band has been used to protect the striking wheel and also cover the bottom and hold in the tinder.

3 **Swiss+Tech keychain multitool.** Swiss+Tech has done a fantastic job of establishing themselves as a keychain multitool company. They make great little tools at affordable prices. The one I included in this kit costs only $5. It includes pliers, wire cutter, wire stripper, sheet shear, flathead screwdriver, and a Phillips screwdriver.

4 **Paracord-wrapped fishing kit.** This mini paracord-wrapped kit includes fishing line, hooks, sinkers, swivels, bobbers, miniknife, cotton fire tinder, and a ferro rod. Similar kits are very easy to make at home. The weave used for the paracord is called the cobra weave. If you search it on YouTube, there are plenty of instructional videos.

5 **Paracord monkey's fist.** You can never have enough 7-strand paracord. This woven keychain contains about 6' of additional paracord. In paracord language, that's 6' × 8 strands, which equals 48' of usable cordage.

6 **LED keychain light.** These small, lightweight LED flashlights are the perfect addition to keychain survival kits. It's amazing how much light these little guys throw out.

EDC ON A BUDGET KIT #5: THE PARACORD BRACELET KIT

I have seen many paracord bracelet survival kits over the years, and I am constantly amazed at how many resources can be packed into them.

CONTAINER:

WOVEN PARACORD BRACELET

All of the tools and resources in this kit are either woven inside or attached to the exterior of a standard paracord survival bracelet. Similar to the paracord fishing kit mentioned in the Keychain Kit in this chapter, most paracord bracelets are woven using the cobra weave.

CONTENTS

1 **Paracord.** The average paracord bracelet has 8'–10' of 7-strand paracord. The outer sheath plus the 7 inner strands totals 64'–80' of survival cordage, which can be used for all kinds of survival functions from fishing line and snare sets to shelter lashings and gear repairs.

2 **Ferro rod with striker.** The buckle of this bracelet includes a small ferro rod and striker, which can be used to start a fire in even the worst environments.

3 **Whistle.** The buckle of this bracelet also incorporates a whistle, which can be used as a signaling tool.

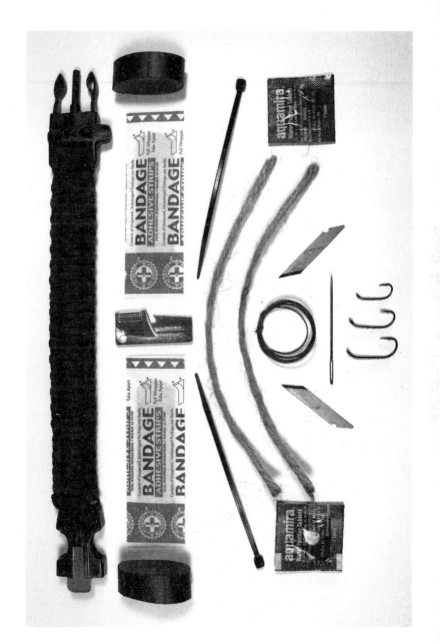

4 P-38. This is a small military can opener. Opening cans of food without a can opener isn't as easy as you might imagine. This is attached to the outside of the bracelet, using Ranger bands.

5 2 Ranger bands. Ranger bands are crosscut sections of bicycle inner tube. These are used on this bracelet to attach the P-38 can opener. These can also be used as a fire starter. Inner tube rubber burns very well when started with an open flame. It will not ignite with sparks.

6 Snare wire. Woven inside the bracelet is 18" of snare wire. This can be used to make a small-game snare.

7 Wax-coated jute twine. Woven inside the bracelet are 2 6" strands of wax-coated jute twine. Jute twine is an amazing plant-fiber fire starter. The wax coating helps waterproof it and also makes it burn longer and stronger.

8 Needle. Woven inside the bracelet is a large sail needle. This is mainly for gear repair and can be hacked and used as an awl as shown in the Improvised Needle Awl hack in Chapter 6. Use with the inner strands of paracord as thread.

9 Bandages. Two small bandages are woven inside of the bracelet. These can be used for minor first-aid emergencies.

10 Water purification tablets. Woven inside the bracelet are 2 water purification tablets. These can be used with scavenged containers to chemically purify wild water.

11 2 knife blades. Woven inside the bracelet are 2 small hobby knife blades. These can be used for small carving/cutting tasks but also make suitable small-game arrowheads.

12 **3 fish hooks.** Woven inside the bracelet are 3 different-sized fish hooks. These can be used in conjunction with the paracord inner strands to catch fish, turtles, birds, or small game. *Note*: In survival, fish hooks aren't just for fish.

13 **2 zip ties.** Zip ties have all kinds of uses. From gear repairs to survival trapping, they're just too lightweight and low profile not to include in a paracord bracelet weaving project.

EDC ON A BUDGET KIT #6: THE SHOE SOLE KIT

This is another minimalist collection of items, with the caveat that everything has to be flat enough to fit under the soles of a pair of hiking boots.

CONTAINER:
SHOES—UNDER-THE-SOLE INSERTS

In my experience, the sole inserts of most hiking boots are thick enough to mask all of the items listed below. In fact, I've had most of them in my shoes for the past several years and often forget they're there. Every item in this kit must be completely (or really close to) flat.

CONTENTS

1 **6' fishing line.** I took a 6" × 2" piece of duct tape and meticulously curled 6' of fishing line in a spiral pattern on the sticky side. Then I applied this to the underside of my shoe sole. This keeps the line in place, and I also have 6" of duct tape, which has many survival uses on its own.

2 **Fresnel lens.** This paper-thin magnifying card can be used to create a solar ember that can be placed into a tinder bundle and blown into flame. These are available for just a couple bucks at any pharmacy. Here's a video of me demonstrating how to use one: *www.willowhaven outdoor.com/punky-wood-video.*

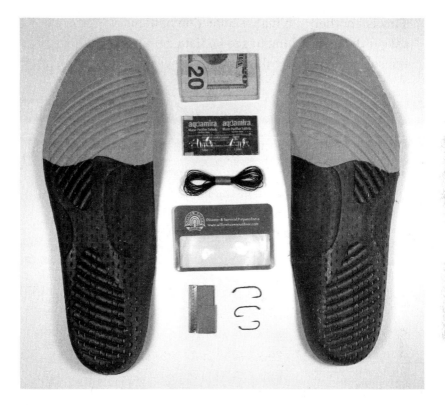

3 **Fish hooks.** Similar to the fishing line, I duct-taped 3 different-sized fishing hooks to the bottom of my shoe sole. This keeps them in place, and you'll never even know they're there.

4 **$20.** You just never know when you might need a few extra bucks.

5 **Razor blade.** Again, the razor blade is duct-taped to the bottom of the shoe sole. This prevents it from moving. Leave the cardboard sleeve on for added protection, both for the blade and for your shoe. The blade can be used for a variety of small-scale survival cutting functions, from trimming fishing line to cleaning small game and even carving small trap or fire kits.

6 **2 water purification tablets.** A very thin, prepackaged envelope of 2 water purification tablets can be easily taped to the bottom of your shoe sole with no issues at all. The packaging is sealed, which prevents moisture damage.

EDC ON A BUDGET KIT #7: THE CELL PHONE BELT POUCH KIT

In a world where everyone has a cell phone, a very nondescript survival kit can easily be disguised. When people see a cell phone pouch, they automatically assume that a cell phone is inside. This will be our little secret.

CONTAINER:
ANY KIND OF CELL PHONE BELT POUCH

Cell phone belt pouches come in an infinite number of shapes and sizes. They also make the perfect container for a small travel-sized survival kit.

CONTENTS

1 50" duct tape. I meticulously rolled 50" of duct tape into a small 2" × ¾" log. The survival applications are endless.

2 Slingshot bands. A set of small-game-hunting slingshot bands available for just a few bucks at almost all outdoor sports retailers are included in this kit. From squirrels and rabbits to pigeons and rats, the slingshot will always be one of my favorite survival small-game-hunting tools. A natural tree fork and smooth rocks can be used to complete the ensemble.

3 Ursa Major Essential Face Wipe. This wet wipe by Ursa Major was given to me by a friend and makes a perfect hygiene addition to a travel-belt kit. Use it to wash hands, take a spit bath, or clean gear.

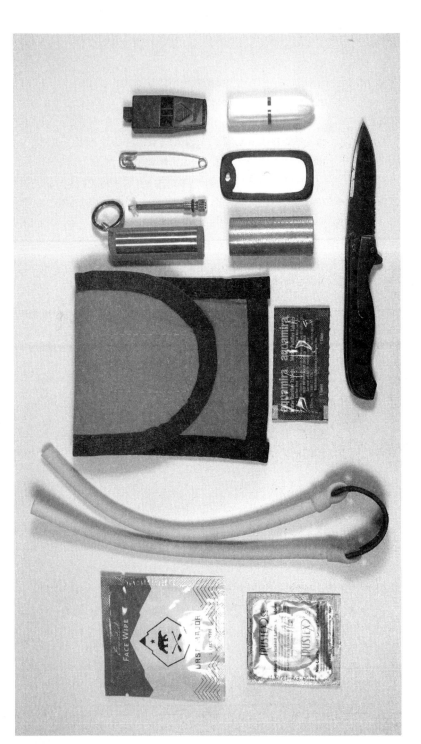

4 Whistle. A whistle travels farther, is louder, and requires less energy than using your voice to signal for rescue.

5 Nonlubricated condom. You can fill this with 1 liter of drinking water. Use it in conjunction with water purification tablets (mentioned next) to purify wild water. It can also be filled with water, formed into a sphere, and used to magnify the sun's rays to start a fire.

6 2 water purification tablets. Each tablet is good for 1 liter of water. These can be used with the condom to purify water.

7 Forever match. This forever match is fueled with lighter fluid, but even if that runs out you can use the mini ferro rod striker to start a fire in dry tinder.

8 Safety pin. Safety pins are great for a variety of gear repairs in the field.

9 Cotton tampon. A plastic-wrapped, organic cotton tampon makes the perfect compact supply of fire tinder.

10 Dog tag signal mirror. This mini signal mirror can be used to reflect the sun's rays and signal for rescue if necessary.

11 Folding knife. A cell phone case is large enough to support a nice-sized folding knife that has an infinite number of uses for everyday tasks or survival functions.

Conclusion

These 7 hack kits just scratch the surface of what is possible in the realm of EDC survival kit hacking. Your imagination is your only limit. I am amazed every day at the creative survival solutions and ideas that I see from friends, students, survival enthusiasts, and fellow instructors. It confirms what I've been saying the past 20 years—*Innovation is the most important survival skill*! May your skills be solid and your hacks be many.

Remember, it's not *if* but *when*.

Acknowledgments

I'd like to thank my Father in heaven for loving me despite my flaws and for forgiving me when I fail him and others. I deserve neither. I'd like to thank the countless individuals who have supported my career in the self-reliance industry by training with me at willowhavenout door.com and escapethewoods.com, purchasing my books, ordering from notifbutwhensurvivalstore.com, subscribing to myapocabox.com, and watching *Fat Guys in the Woods* on the Weather Channel. If you are one of these individuals, my sincerest thank you. I'd also like to thank the Boy Scouts of America for teaching me early in life that a Scout is trustworthy, loyal, helpful, friendly, courteous, kind, obedient, cheerful, thrifty, brave, clean, and reverent. I will continue to aspire to be all of these things; "aspire" being the key word in this sentence.

Index